ADVENT and LENTEN Studies

For use in Christian Study & Discussion Groups

HUBERT J. SMITH

The Canterbury Press
Norwich

© Hubert J. Smith 1995

First published 1995 by The Canterbury Press Norwich
(a publishing imprint of Hymns Ancient & Modern Limited,
a registered charity)
St Mary's Works, St Mary's Plain,
Norwich, Norfolk, NR3 3BH

*All rights reserved. No part of this publication which is copyright may
be reproduced, stored in a retrieval system, or transmitted, in any form
or by any means, electronic, mechanical, photocopying, recording, or
otherwise, without the prior permission of the publisher.*

Hubert J. Smith has asserted his right under the Copyright, Designs
and Patents Act, 1988, to be identified as Author of this Work

British Library Cataloguing in Publication Data

A catalogue record for this book is available
from the British Library

ISBN 1-85311-121-X

*Typeset by David Gregson Associates,
Beccles, Suffolk
and printed in Great Britain
by Bell and Bain Ltd, Glasgow*

By the same author:
EXPLORING THE CHRISTIAN FAITH (1994)

PRELIMINARY NOTES

The following Studies are intended to serve as a series of short introductions to Advent and Lenten themes, designed to be used as 'starters' for further investigation, and to provoke debate. The aim is to provide local congregations (or interchurch groups) with a programme which will facilitate the sharing of ideas and insights during the seasons of Advent and Lent. These periods in the Christian calendar, by tradition, have been set aside for this kind of reflection, but it has been the experience of most groups that some clear structure is needed if this reflection is to be productive.

Why bring Advent and Lent together in a single publication? Because in reality the two are inseparable. It is one of the fundamental principles of Christian theology that the incarnation of God in Christ cannot be disconnected from his death and resurrection. His person and his work go together. It is therefore hoped that church groups will take this fact seriously, and treat this book as a coherent whole, rather than as 'two books in one'. However, the material has been structured so that, if necessary, the Advent and the Lenten themes can be approached independently. This has resulted in a slight degree of repetition at those points where the two necessarily overlap, but this will not prove to be a difficulty in practice.

There are eight Studies in each of the two sections of the book, but groups are free to select from them as they wish, and to adapt the material to suit their own needs and circumstances.

It is strongly recommended that every member of the group shall have his/her own copy of this book, so that the material contained in the introductory Studies can be read and digested before the meetings actually take place. This is likely to be far more effective than the common practice of placing a single copy of the book in the hands of the group Leader, leaving everyone else to wait until the meeting before giving the issues any thought.

There should also be copies of the Bible available at each meeting. Every Study contains Scriptural references, and these are intended to be examined during the course of the discussion. Any version of the Bible will serve, and there is much to be said for making several different translations available so that comparisons can be made. The Biblical passages quoted in the Studies themselves are taken from the **New Revised Standard Version** (Oxford University Press 1989).

At the end of each Study there is a short list of points for discussion. These have been included to ensure that the group does not run out of ideas, and to keep the debate closely linked to the particular subject-area. But of course it is open to every group to follow its own inclinations in raising whatever issues seem to be relevant. It is more than likely that the discussion topics will prove to be the most worthwhile parts of the entire book, with the introductory Studies serving simply as background information and as stimulants to thought.

In the Studies themselves, contemporary scholarship has been taken fully into account. Such matters as the historicity of the narratives about the birth of Christ, or the doctrine of the Virgin Birth, or the nature of Christ's resurrection are all opened up for consideration. No doubt those who use this book will come to a wide variety of conclusions, but the discipline of wrestling with such questions is exactly what Advent and Lent are intended to encourage. They are seasons of soul-searching, and as such they invite every Christian to engage in an honest quest for truth, no matter how controversial the questions might be.

CONTENTS

Preliminary Notes   page iii

Advent Studies

1. **God With Us**   5
2. **Humanity as the Image of God**   13
3. **The Messianic Hope**   20
4. **Matthew's Birth Narrative**   28
5. **Luke's Birth Narrative**   35
6. **The Word Became Flesh**   44
7. **The Incarnation in Paul's Theology**   51
8. **The Celebration of Christmas**   58

Lenten Studies

1. **Corporate Humanity**   67
2. **Pain and Suffering**   74
3. **Justice, Mercy and Forgiveness**   82
4. **Sacrifice**   89
5. **Obedience**   96
6. **The Death of Christ**   102
7. **The Resurrection of Christ**   108
8. **Risen With Christ**   116

Index of Biblical References   122

ADVENT STUDIES

1 God With Us

The season of Advent was introduced into the western Church calendar, probably in the sixth century, as an opportunity for Christians to reflect upon the significance of the Incarnation, so that when the birth of Christ is celebrated at Christmas, there might be a clearer awareness of its meaning. In this opening Advent Study we shall begin by exploring one of the central themes, not only of Christmas, but also of the Bible as a whole – that of the 'immanence of God', because it is this idea which lies at the very heart of the Christian doctrine of the Incarnation.

The word 'immanence' means 'to dwell within', and in the Christian sense it has to do with the belief that God is permanently present within his own creation. It should not be confused with the word 'imminence', which means 'to be near or close', because that is a very different matter. We are not speaking of a God who is about to be present, or who is intending to enter our experience at some future time: we are speaking of a God who is already 'with us'.

Although the Old Testament certainly does contain ideas of God which emphasise his 'otherness' and seem to place him 'out there', remote and unreachable, there are also numerous other passages in which the writers bear witness to their conviction that God is somehow close at hand. For example, in the narrative of creation *(Genesis 2:4ff)* God is described as making the heavens and the earth, and then crowning his work by making a human being, who is placed in a paradisical garden to be responsible for looking after it. After the work of creation is completed, God is then said to 'walk in the garden' during the cool of the evening *(Genesis 3:8)*, almost in the manner of a gardener who, after a busy day, enjoys what he has done. Here we have a delightful piece of ancient religious mythology which testifies to a conviction that the God who made the universe does not stand apart from it, in splendid isolation, but actually enters into it and enjoys it. He even engages in direct conversation with the human beings he has created. He talks with his people, and listens to what they have to say.

We find similar ideas expressed in the Psalms of the Old Testament, which might be described as the devotional literature of ancient Israel. Once again, although God is sometimes pictured as being distant or high above the earth – as, for example, in Psalm 2, where he is described as sitting in the heavens *(Psalm 2:4)*, or in Psalm 10, where the writer feels that God is standing far off *(Psalm 10:1)* – he is also experienced as being very close. The author of Psalm 18 speaks of God reaching down and taking hold of him *(Psalm 18:16)*, and the magnificent Psalm 23 portrays God as a caring shepherd who is with his flock even in the most difficult and dangerous situations *(Psalm 23:4)*. The very nature of the Psalms themselves is also evidence of a widespread belief that God can hear his people when they speak to him, and that he can and will respond.

Pantheism and Panentheism

But this belief in an immanent God is certainly not the same thing as Pantheism. Pantheism is a belief that God *is* everything, and that everything is God. It identifies God with his creation, and produces nature-worship, based on the notion that the universe, and all that it contains, are in themselves divine. According to this theory, God and the universe are identical. Nor is it the same thing as Panentheism. Panentheism (a term coined in the early nineteenth century) suggests that God somehow contains everything within himself, so that the created universe becomes a part of him, though not all of him, because he is more than what he has made.

How can God be both far and near?

At first sight it looks as if a belief in an immanent God directly contradicts the idea of a God who is, as the famous hymn of W. Chalmers Smith put it:

'Immortal, invisible, God only wise,
in light inaccessible, hid from our eyes',

but the fact that these two concepts can quite easily exist side by side in the Old Testament invites us to look at them more closely to see if there really is a contradiction.

In Psalm 8 the writer contemplates the night sky, and wonders how it could possibly be true that the God who made the moon and the stars should bother to take an interest in such insignificant little things as human beings *(Psalm 8:3–4)*. Here, the psalmist is reflecting something of the seeming paradox of a God who is both 'up there' and also 'down here'. In much the same way, the author of Psalm 139 pours out his feelings about a God who is so close to him that every part of him is intimately known, yet who is also so universal in his nature that no-one can hide from him *(Psalm 139:1–18)*. This God is able to have an intimate and complete knowledge of every single individual, and yet also be everywhere – even where no-one has ever yet been. The seeming contradiction is resolved by affirming the universality of God, for whom nothing is impossible and to whom all things are known.

God's involvement in human affairs

Not only is it affirmed that God is both outside and inside the created order: it is also said that God is actually involved in earthly events, controlling and directing them. He has not simply made the world and then left it alone to 'tick over' on its own, independently of him. He can and does intervene. He is a God who is always active and alert, who continually does things, and people can even see him at work. He takes hold of individuals and gives them things to do, as, for example, in the story of Moses at the Burning Bush *(Exodus 3:1ff)*. God speaks to Moses, and explains that he has chosen him to go to the Egyptian Pharaoh, to bring the people of Israel out of slavery and take them to a new land. Although, for the sake of religious convention, this narrative carefully avoids saying that Moses actually set eyes on God, it is clear that this represents a close and very personal encounter between a man and God.

A similar kind of encounter is said to have been experienced by the young Samuel *(I Samuel 3:1ff)*. When he was lying down in his room in the sacred precincts where the Ark of the Covenant was kept, he heard God's voice calling to him *(I Samuel 3:2–14)*. At first he thought it was the voice of the old priest Eli, but then he realised that it was God who was warning him of an impending punishment which would fall upon Eli's family. Although the story is told in a quaintly childlike fashion, it reflects the common and profound Old Testament belief that God was well aware of what was going on among his people, and that he was prepared to intervene when things were not to his liking. He had delegated responsibility, but he was still in control.

Seeing God

Although as we have noted, there are many Old Testament passages which affirm that God is constantly present with his people, one of the most insistent themes of the Bible is that no ordinary human being has ever set eyes directly on God. Even Moses himself was afraid to look at him *(Exodus 3:1–6)*, and the writer of the narrative takes pains to say that it was an 'angel of God' which appeared in the Burning Bush. The same convention of language is used later on, in the story of the freed Israelite slaves making their way out of Egypt, pursued by the Egyptian chariots. As the people make their escape, it is again 'the angel of God' who goes in front of them, and then moves behind them to thwart the following army *(Exodus 14:19–20)*, and the actual presence of God is described as being in the form of a pillar of cloud. This way of writing came about as a result of the aversion of the ancient Hebrews to any suggestion that there could be a direct physical encounter taking place between human beings and God. To see God was to risk instant death *(Exodus 19:21)*, and to make contact with him would bring disaster. Even to tread on God's ground would bring death, because the trespasser would be infected with God's personal holiness; the penalty was to be executed by stoning or by being shot with arrows, so that the executioner would not have to touch the offender and thus also become contaminated *(Exodus 19:12–13)*.

But seeing is not limited to physical sight. There is such a thing as 'insight', and here we touch upon one of the most subtle and most important of all Biblical ideas. The distinction is well expressed in the book of Deuteronomy in the Old Testament:

> *'Moses summoned all Israel and said to them: You have seen all that the LORD did before your eyes in the land of Egypt, to Pharaoh and to all his servants and to all his land, the great trials that your eyes saw, the signs and those great wonders. But to this day the LORD has not given you a mind to understand, or eyes to see, or ears to hear ...'*
> *(Deuteronomy 29:2–4)*

The point is that in order to see God's self-revelation clearly, one must not only look at what is going on, but also look into it. It is this capacity to see beyond the outward physical appearance, into what lies within, that constitutes true sight. Religious perception is the key. It is not merely a question of looking in the right place for God; it is much more a matter of looking in the right way.

In the New Testament there are two stories about seeing, placed side by side in the Gospel of Mark. In the first narrative *(Mark 8:22–26)*, Jesus heals an anonymous blind man. He does this in two stages, and at first the man can see only partially. Then, after a second touch by Jesus, he sees clearly. This account is followed immediately by another story – this time about Jesus questioning his followers as to what they think of him. How do people see him? At first, there is only a partial awareness that he is special. Then Jesus asks a second time, and now the answer is clear: Peter recognises him as the expected Messiah *(Mark 8:27–30)*, the Son of God. Further evidence of a link between the two stories is provided by the fact that the blind man in the first narrative comes from Bethsaida: and, according to John 1:44, that also was the birthplace of Peter. What Mark seems to be saying is that Peter was himself the blind man who received the gift of true sight. Biblically speaking, therefore, 'seeing' God is a religious matter, and is not to be confused with the physical quest to 'set eyes' on him. To be able to recognise God within the ordinary circumstances and events of life was the most important thing. It was this which marked out the special gifts of the great prophets, who were men who possessed religious insight.

Prophetic insight

Even a brief study of the books of the prophets in the Old Testament is sufficient to show that they were ordinary men with extraordinary gifts. Above all, they were able to 'see and hear' God. It was not that God had somehow chosen to approach them differently from all others: it was that they had a sensitivity which others generally lacked. They saw the same things that other people saw, but they looked more deeply into them. The prophet Isaiah, for example, looked at the political situation as it was in the eighth century before Christ, but he saw much more than the outward signs of impending invasion. He saw what was happening as evidence of God's personal intervention, and he was able to put the political issues into a religious context. In just the same way, the prophet Jeremiah looked at the events of his own time, and was able to probe more deeply into their religious significance. Even the most unimportant things seemed to have a special meaning: in the opening chapter of his book the prophet recounts how he looked at the branch of an almond tree, and then at a boiling pot which was tilted away from the north, and found in them a deeper truth *(Jeremiah 1:11–19)*. This was also the experience of the prophet Amos, who drew religious insight from watching a plague of locusts destroying a field, and from seeing a basket full of summer fruit *(Amos 7:1ff and 8:1–3).*

What comes out of all this is the realisation that, throughout the Bible, God is perceived as being present or immanent within the experience of human beings. His creative power is clearly evidenced by the created universe itself, but his actual purposes (and even to some extent his nature) can also be 'seen' by those who are prepared to use their God-given powers of insight. His word can be 'heard' by those who have ears to hear. The Law (or, more correctly, the TORAH) contains his guidance, and the prophets deliver his condemnations and warnings in the light of that Law. He is not an absentee God, but a God who shares the world with his people, and knows their joys and their sufferings. These Biblical insights provide the foundation for the Christian affirmation that God entered most fully into human experience by actually taking on humanity itself – and we come to this point in our next Study.

POINTS FOR DISCUSSION

1. Is the eternal majesty of God placed at risk if we think of him as being immanent? Are we in danger of reducing his divine status?
2. Are there limits to the claim that God is 'in' everything that takes place? What would be the consequences for Christian belief if we were to say that there are certain areas of experience from which God is absent, or which are somehow beneath him?
3. If a special kind of religious insight is necessary in order to 'see' God, does this imply that some people are incapable of achieving this, and must remain forever 'blind'?
4. If every event is capable of being understood as deriving from God, and as evidence of his involvement in human affairs, is it proper to blame him as well as praise him?
5. Are there any dangers inherent in the idea that God's word can be understood best by those with special insight?

Could this lead to the emergence of an elite religious group who know the truth about God better than others?

6. If God is 'immanent' in the way we have described, what might be the evidence of his presence within human beings? How could we distinguish between the things that are 'of God' and those which are not?

2 | Humanity as the Image of God

This second Study takes us on a further step from our consideration of the 'immanence' of God, and invites us to focus more directly upon the Biblical teaching about the special relationship between God and human beings.

The place of mankind in God's creation

Throughout this discussion we shall use the conventional word 'mankind' to include both the male and the female genders. This is in no way to perpetuate the idea that men are superior to women: it is simply a recognition that this is how human beings are generally referred to in the Christian Scriptures.

According to the two narratives of creation in the book of Genesis *(Genesis 1:1—2:4a, and 2:4b—3:24)*, mankind was the crowning achievement of God's creative work. In the first account (which was almost certainly written considerably later than the second, and seems to come from the context of religious Temple liturgy), God first creates light and separates it from the primeval darkness. He then creates the universe itself, putting the earth in place and filling it with vegetation and living creatures. The final creative act is that of making human beings, and giving them authority over everything that the universe contains. Thus, in this progressive series of events, mankind is the 'final touch' – the supreme ruler under God of the world that he has made. Everything is said to be 'very good', that is, all is in full accord with God's creative intention, and God is then able to regard creation as completed.

In the second story of creation we encounter a very different style of writing. This is a childlike piece of mythology (using that word in its proper sense), in which very subtle ideas are set out in simple but telling language. Yet, although the style is so different from the previous narrative, it is again clear that mankind is regarded as God's supreme creation, Here, man is the first living being to inhabit the newly-made earth. A beautiful garden is provided for his physical and aesthetic needs, though he is warned that he must not break the limits of his freedom by taking what is not rightly his. There is one tree in the garden which he must not touch, and from which he must not eat the fruits. Then God sets about finding the man some suitable company, because it is in the nature of the human individual that he is not a solitary being. He is gregarious. So the animals and the birds are made, and the man is given authority over them, but they do not meet his deepest need for a partner. Finally a woman is made, and the mode of her appearance (she is shaped from the man's own body) indicates her affinity to him. The man and woman are 'one'.

We do not need here to go into all the details of this magnificent imagery: what we should note is the status which mankind is given in both of these otherwise very different narratives. Mankind is the crowning achievement of creation. The same idea appears in other parts of the Bible: we have already noted the sentiments of Psalm 8, where the writer says

> '... *what are human beings that you are mindful of them, mortals that you care for them? Yet you have made them a little lower than God, and crowned them with glory and honour ...: (Psalm 8:4–5)*

But here, in the creation narratives, we find the astonishing claim that mankind is actually made to match God:

> '*Then God said, "Let us make humankind in our image, according to our likeness:"* ' *(Genesis 1:26ff)*

This goes far beyond the belief that mankind is superior to the rest of creation. It openly gives human beings the status of being Godlike.

Like God, or like the animals?

Before we go any further, it is worthwhile to observe that in modern times this man-centred view of the universe has been seriously challenged. Theories of evolution have insisted that human beings are, in reality, animals themselves, with biological similarities and other characteristics which bind humanity firmly together, not with God, but with the animal kingdom. It is this which caused so much offence in the nineteenth century, when Darwinism compelled Christian thinkers to think again about their claims to be superior to every other living thing. Yet general experience had already prompted the more sensitive members of society to doubt man's divine perfection: the eighteenth century writer Alexander Pope had this to say about man:

> *'A being darkly wise, and rudely great:*
> *With too much knowledge for the sceptic side,*
> *With too much weakness for the stoic's pride,*
> *He hangs between; in doubt to act or rest,*
>
> *In doubt to deem himself a god, or beast;*
> *In doubt his mind or body to prefer,*
> *Born but to die, and reas'ning but to err;*
> *Alike in ignorance, his reason such,*
> *Whether he thinks too little or too much ...*
>
> *Created half to rise, and half to fall;*
> *Great lord of all things, yet a prey to all;*
> *Sole judge of truth, in endless error hurled;*
> *The glory, jest, and riddle of the world!'*
> (Alexander Pope, **An Essay on Man**, Epistle 2)

The 'Fall' of man and the Adam saga

This recognition that mankind is somehow flawed is evident in the second and older creation myth. Here, the writer attributes it to something which has traditionally become known as 'the Fall'. In Genesis chapter 3 we find the story of mankind's disobedience of God's law: the man had been told that he could live in, and enjoy the paradisical garden, but that he must not eat nor even touch the fruit of the tree of the knowledge of good and evil. If he disobeys, then he will die. But he and the woman are tempted, and they eat. Their offence is known to God, who does not take their lives, but instead he condemns them to a life which will include suffering, and he also locks them out of the garden, guarding the tree so that they cannot reach it.

This is magnificent imagery, subtle in the extreme, and presented not as a piece of factual history but as an analysis of the human condition. Man, by his self-will, has broken the special relationship with God which was given to him, and now stands in a position of alienation. It is in the hands of God as to whether that relationship can ever be restored.

The imagery of the 'Fall' is taken up by St Paul in the New Testament, when he is describing both the nature and the work of Jesus Christ. In his letter to the Philippians he portrays Christ as the 'new man', made in the form (or 'image') of God, but, unlike the first man, able to resist the temptation to become equal to God:

> *'... though he was in the form of God, (he) did not regard equality with God as something to be exploited, but emptied himself, taking the form of a slave, being born in human likeness.*
>
> *And being found in human form, he humbled himself, and became obedient to the point of death – even death on a cross ...' (Philippians 2:6ff)*

The parallel with the Genesis story is obvious. Where the 'first' man failed, the 'new' man succeeded. Here is a new act of creation, but this time mankind's disobedience is replaced by obedience, and the relationship with God is not broken, but sustained. Again, in his letter to the Colossians, Paul describes Jesus as

> *'the image of the invisible God, the firstborn of all creation' (Colossians 1:15),*

once more making a direct allusion to the creation story of Genesis.

In his letter to the church in Rome, Paul yet again pictures Jesus as the new mankind (which is what the name 'Adam' really signifies). Jesus goes through the 'Adam' experience, but he does not offend against God's law. Whereas Adam's offence resulted in divine punishment for all who shared human nature, the work of Jesus resulted not in death but in new life:

> *'If, because of the one man's trespass, death exercised dominion through that one, much more surely will those who receive the abundance of grace and the free gift of righteousness exercise dominion in life through the one man, Jesus Christ.'*
> *(Romans 5:17)*

The same idea is made explicit in Paul's correspondence with the Corinthian church:

> *'... for as all die in Adam, so all will be made alive in Christ.'*
> *(I Corinthians 15:22)*

The Humanity of Christ

For a Christian, all this points towards the necessity to recognise Christ as a true human being. He is the 'image of God', but at the same time he is also 'Adam', the symbol of humanity. If St Paul's theology is to be accepted, and the work of Jesus really is the start of a new act of creation, then it is essential to accept Jesus's full humanity. His birth is in itself a fresh start for the human race, and this why the New Testament contains so many allusions to Christian belief as a way into a new life. It is in effect the restoration of the image of God in mankind.

Yet throughout the Christian centuries there has been something of a reluctance to take the true humanity of Jesus seriously. The fear that his divine nature will somehow be reduced by acknowledging his humanity has resulted in various manifestations of the ancient Gnostic teaching known as **Docetism**.

Docetism was a somewhat vague philosophy, current in the days of the early Church, which taught that Jesus's humanity was not real, but only an outward appearance which he adopted for reasons of convenience. According to this outlook, Jesus went through the motions of seeming to be a real human being, but those who were possessed of special inside knowledge (the 'Gnostics') were able to recognise his true divine nature. The consequence of this, however, was that in order to sustain this teaching it became necessary to deny that Jesus really suffered on the Cross and that he died a physical death. Thus it led also to a rejection of the central Christian doctrine of the Resurrection, and Docetism was condemned as a heresy by later Christian authorities. But it is an idea which has never quite disappeared, and even today it is not uncommon to find statements made about Jesus which have the effect of turning him into kind of 'superman' – human, yet not quite as human as the rest of mankind.

Several years ago a television play by Denis Potter, entitled **Son of Man**, provoked storms of protest from viewers who disliked the way in which Jesus was portrayed as something of an eccentric figure, dishevelled in appearance and apparently uncertain of his mission and even of himself. The protesters insisted that the 'real' Jesus could not possibly have been like that, because he was the Son of God, and therefore had to be 'a cut above everyone else'. Yet to make Christ superhuman is to miss the whole point of the Incarnation: the writer of the letter to the Hebrews in the New Testament put the issue very clearly: although his approach is to see Jesus, not as the new Adam but as the supreme High Priest, he fully appreciated that God's purpose could not be achieved unless Christ was fully human:

> *'For we do not have a high priest who is unable to sympathize with our weaknesses, but we have one who in every respect has been tempted (or "tested") as we are, yet without sin ...'.*
> *(Hebrews 4:15)*

In the same way, the author of the Fourth Gospel insists that the Incarnation was real, and that Jesus was not an apparition but a fully human person who, like all other human beings, was flesh and blood, yet was still able to make God known *(John 1:14–18)*.

POINTS FOR DISCUSSION

1. Compare the two Creation stories in Genesis (1:1 to 2:4a, and 2:4b to 3:24). Do they give human beings the same status in relation to God?

2. What does the ban on 'eating of the tree of the knowledge of good and evil' mean? Does it suggest that, without God, human beings are incapable of knowing right from wrong?

3. In what sense do we all share in the consequences of 'the Fall of Adam'? Or is this an outmoded idea?

4. Do you agree with St Paul's description of what people are like when they are alienated from God (see Romans 1:18–32)? Is he being too hard on us?

5. If Jesus was truly a human being like all of us, what does the writer of the letter to the Hebrews mean when he adds that Jesus was 'without sin' (see Hebrews 4:15)? Does this not separate him from 'fallen' humanity, and make him altogether different?

6. Do you agree with the television viewers who were offended at the idea that Jesus might have been physically unattractive, or eccentric in his behaviour? Has Christian art sometimes seemed to remove Jesus from ordinary life and made him seem unreal, or even 'too good to be true'?

3 The Messianic Hope

Throughout the New Testament Jesus is referred to as 'the Christ', which is the Greek form of the Hebrew word 'Messiah', meaning 'God's Anointed One'. Indeed, the title 'Christ' is so closely identified with Jesus that it becomes part of his name (as in 'Jesus Christ' or 'Christ Jesus'), or even the whole of it, when the name 'Jesus' is omitted altogether and he is simply called 'Christ' *(see, for example, Romans 5:6, 6:9, 7:4, 8:9–11 and many other places)*. This is such a familiar way of speaking about Jesus that its significance is frequently overlooked, and in this Study we shall consider something of what it means.

We have to begin by going back to Old Testament times, because it was from their past history as Jews that the earliest Christians derived their understanding of the Messiah.

The need for a future hope

The first significant point to note is that throughout their history the Hebrew people have had to endure a great deal of suffering and persecution. One of the reasons for this has been geographical: their country is positioned very vulnerably between two great land masses which used to contain the Empires of Mesopotamia and Asia Minor in the north, and of Egypt to the south. They were therefore always at risk of invasion, because Palestine (as the whole country was then generally known) formed a crucially important bridgehead between these great powers. Furthermore, they were constantly subjected to the cultural as well as the political pressures applied by those who invaded their land – the Persians, the Greeks, and then the Romans in particular: such pressures put their own religious beliefs and practices in jeopardy, and there was an almost permanent anxiety among many Israelite people that they might lose their identity and become swallowed up by forces much stronger than themselves. They needed to work out ways of protecting their traditions, and at the same time they clung steadfastly to the religious hope that there would come a day when they would be free to become what they were – the people of God. So their geography profoundly affected their history, and their history influenced their religious hopes and aspirations. It was often in times of political unrest or danger of invasion that the great prophets of Old Testament times would deliver what they believed to be the word of God, and it was out of their message that the hope of a coming Messiah was largely formulated.

We can see something of this kind of hope clearly expressed in the words of Zacharias (or Zechariah) the priest (Luke 1:68–75), rejoicing after the birth of John the Baptist:

> *'Blessed be the Lord God of Israel, for he has looked favourably on his people and redeemed them. He has raised up a mighty saviour for us in the house of his servant David, as he spoke through the mouth of his holy prophets from of old, that we would be saved from our enemies and from the hand of all who hate us ...' (Luke 1:68–71)*

But what would that Messiah be like? How would he be recognised when he finally came? And when would he arrive? These were crucially important questions. To answer them, the Old Testament community found a variety of possibilities. Some of them were directly linked with the religious belief that there would one day be an end to history or to time itself, when God would fulfil all his promises, and take his rightful place as 'King of Kings'. Teachings of this sort are commonly referred to by scholars as **eschatological**, because they have to do with 'the last days' (in the Greek language, the 'eschatos'), when God's kingdom (or, more correctly, his 'kingship') would be established. Other teachings, however, were associated with more directly political or military hopes. We can glance at some of the most prominent ideas which the Old Testament contains, all of which involve an important element of hopeful anticipation.

The new Moses

For many, the Messianic hope grew out of remembered history, with the expectation that one day God would again do what he had already done: he would intervene personally in human affairs, as he had done when the ancient Hebrew people were enslaved in Egypt. Just as he had sent Moses to rescue them from oppression under a tyrannical Pharaoh, so God would raise up a new Moses to re-enact the great Exodus. Thus the hoped-for Messiah would be like Moses, or even 'Moses-come-again', in that he would embody all that Moses had been. Just as the first Moses had been instrumental in the making of the covenant and in the delivery of the laws *(see Exodus 19:1ff and 34:1ff)* this new Moses would establish a new covenant between God and his people, and he would deliver a new Law (Torah). The book of Deuteronomy puts the hope on the lips of Moses himself:

> *'The LORD your God will raise up for you a prophet like me from among your own people; you shall heed such a prophet.'*
> *(Deuteronomy 18:15)*

Again, the same kind of hope is set out clearly in the book of the prophet Jeremiah:

> *'The days are surely coming, says the LORD, when I will make a new covenant with the house of Israel and the house of Judah. It will not be like the covenant that I made with their ancestors when I took them by the hand to bring them out of the land of Egypt – a covenant that they broke ...*
> *I will put my law within them, and I will write it on their hearts; and I will be their God, and they shall be my people.'*
> *(Jeremiah 31:31ff)*

In the New Testament we can see the theme set out not only in the contents but also in the actual structure of the Gospel of Matthew. Evidently the author was convinced that Jesus was inaugurating a new 'age of Moses', and he carefully plans his Gospel to depict Jesus doing what Moses did. Jesus stands on a mountain to deliver a new Law in the form of the Sermon on the Mount *(Matthew 5:1—7:29)*. Even the story of Jesus' birth is told by Matthew in a style which explicitly echoes the Moses saga of the book of Exodus: Jesus is said to have been miraculously preserved from Herod's threats by being taken into Egypt, and then brought out again to symbolise the delivery of the people *(Matthew 2:7–15)*. Herod himself is clearly a kind of symbol of the Egyptian Pharaoh.

Again, St Paul evidently viewed the work of Jesus in the same Moses-context. In his letter to the Romans he speaks of the work of Christ as being that of setting people free from slavery:

> *'Thanks be to God that you, having once been slaves of sin, have become obedient from the heart to the form of teaching to which you were entrusted, and that you, having been set free from sin, have become slaves of righteousness ...'*
> *(Romans 6:17ff)*

> *'For the law of the spirit of life has set you free from the law of sin and death. For God has done what the law, weakened by the flesh, could not do: by sending his own son in the likeness of sinful flesh, and to deal with sin, he condemned sin in the flesh ...' (Romans 8:3)*

It is in passages such as these that we see the strong influence of the Exodus tradition in shaping the expectations of the people of Old Testament times. The idea that God was a 'redeeming' deity was always at the forefront of their minds. Whatever their predicament, be it national or personal, such a God would not leave them without hope, but, in his own time, he would step in and save them.

The throne of David

But there was another even more powerful influence upon the Messianic thinking of the Jews, and that was the memory of the great King David (died c.970 BC), who ruled over the united tribes of Israel and Judah. According to Jewish tradition, David was the man upon whom God had placed the mantle of divine kingship. He was the youngest son of Jesse, and was probably born in Bethlehem. Oddly, in view of the remarkable reputation which David acquired within Judaism, his name is hardly ever found in any writings or inscriptions outside the Bible. But in the Old Testament his reign is described in considerable detail, and his own personal history is also related in a way which suggests that the information was derived from a source which was very close to him. His political achievements were astonishing, including not only the final suppression of the Philistine threat but also his capturing of the city of Jerusalem, which became known both as the city of David and also as the Holy City, because it was the place where the first Jewish Temple was erected.

David's reign was not exactly a time of peace, but it was certainly a time of development and of prosperity. It has been likened by some to the age of Queen Elizabeth I in England. Later generations have evidently 'embroidered' some of the legends about David's achievements, but there is undoubtedly a foundation of truth in the tradition that he did more to establish Judaism than any other man. Out of these remembrances there grew up the belief that the future hope of Israel lay in the continuance of the line of David, and the perpetuation of his monarchy (or his 'throne'):

> *'When your days are fulfilled and you lie down with your ancestors, I will raise up your offspring after you, who shall come forth from your body, and I will establish his kingdom. He shall build a house for my name, and I will establish the throne of his kingdom forever ... I will not take my steadfast love from him, as I took it from Saul, whom I put away from before you. Your house and your kingdom shall be made sure forever before me; your throne shall be established forever.'*
> *(2 Samuel 7:12ff)*

Historically speaking, this prophecy was not fulfilled. The united Davidic kingdom fell apart after the reign of David's son Solomon, and ten of the original twelve tribes rejected the kingly line of David altogether, leaving only a tiny minority loyal to the tradition. But it was from this minority (the kingdom of Judah) that the Messianic hope came. The prophets put it plainly into words:

> 'On that day I will raise up the booth ('tabernacle') of David that is fallen, and repair its breaches, and raise up its ruins, and rebuild it as in the days of old ...' (Amos 9:11)

> 'Afterwards the Israelites shall return and seek the LORD their God, and David their king ...' (Hosea 3:5)

> 'But they shall serve the LORD their God and David their king, whom I will raise up for them.' (Jeremiah 30:9)

Initially these prophecies almost certainly had to do with the healing of the breach between the divided kingdoms of Israel and Judah, but they came to be applied to the more general expectation of a coming Messianic king, whose work would go far beyond that of re-uniting the two nations:

> 'A shoot shall come out from the stump of Jesse, and a branch shall grow out of his roots. The spirit of the LORD shall rest upon him, the spirit of wisdom and understanding, the spirit of counsel and might, the spirit of knowledge and the fear of the LORD ... The wolf shall live with the lamb, the leopard shall lie down with the kid, the calf and the lion and the fatling together, and a little child shall lead them ...'
> (Isaiah 11:1–16)

> 'The days are surely coming, says the LORD, when I will fulfil the promise I made to the house of Israel and the house of Judah. In those days and at that time I will cause a righteous Branch to spring up for David; and he shall execute justice and righteousness in the land.' (Jeremiah 33:14–15)

This strong emphasis upon the Davidic line of the coming Messiah is very evident in Matthew's account of the birth of Jesus. The opening verse of his Gospel identifies Jesus as the son of David, as also does the following family tree *(Matthew 1:2–16)*, though it is pertinent to note here that according to this genealogy the Davidic line actually runs through Joseph

(Matthew 1:16), who, in the later part of the narrative, is expressly said not to have been Jesus's father. It may be that we must re-interpret the birth story in the light of this seeming contradiction. Certainly Matthew goes out of his way in his Gospel to demonstrate Jesus's identification with David: he records that, like David, Jesus was born in Bethlehem *(Matthew 2:1)*, even though in his adult life Jesus was always known as 'Jesus of Nazareth'. The Gospel of Luke preserves the same Bethlehem tradition, but explains it in the context of a census or registration by the Roman authorities – a detail which scholars have always found somewhat difficult to reconcile with other historical records as far as dates are concerned.

By the time of the New Testament era the Jewish Messianic hope had developed in several directions, some of which were much more religious than others. It was inevitable that under the Roman regime such hopes would rise to the surface in a militaristic or political way, especially after the heroic feats of the Maccabaean period in the second century BC, when one family was almost single-handedly responsible for freeing Judaea from the yoke of the Syrians. Several personalities emerged who were thought at some point to be candidates for Messiahship, and among them was John the Baptist. In the Gospel of John the author goes to great lengths to show that John was not in fact the Messiah, but was really the 'herald' who, according to Jewish tradition, would appear as a forerunner of the true Messiah and would bear witness to his authenticity *(see John 1:6–9 and 1:19–31)*.

We shall be returning in later Studies to make a closer examination of the various birth narratives of the Gospels, so we need not dwell on them here. The important point at this juncture is to note how it was the Jewish Messianic hopes which provided the context in which Jesus was perceived both during and after his lifetime. To these hopes Jesus himself was to add further important elements, not the least being that of the idea of a Servant-Messiah, who would suffer and die for his people – something which Jews of earlier times would have found utterly inconceivable. But a consideration of that particular aspect must be reserved for our explorations of the Easter theme in the Lenten Studies.

POINTS FOR DISCUSSION

1. In what ways has the Christian religion preserved Judaism's optimism concerning the future? Has Christianity even got a 'future hope'? If so, what is it?
2. Is the present age in need of a new Divine intervention? Or is everything going according to plan?
3. Henry Ford considered that 'history is more or less bunk', and the Russian revolutionary Leon Trotsky called it a 'dustbin'. To what extent is it proper to use past history as a guide to the future? Can we ever know what lies ahead? Does history provide any clues?
4. What do Christians expect to happen when they celebrate the birth of Christ? Is Christmas simply a commemoration of the past?
5. Is a future hope simply wishful thinking? Is there a danger that, by waiting for God to intervene to put the world right, we could shirk our own responsibilities here and now?

4 Matthew's Birth Narrative

There are only two narratives in the New Testament which describe the events surrounding the birth of Christ. One is contained in the Gospel of Matthew, and the other is found in the Gospel of Luke. It has been customary in Christian tradition to merge these two accounts and to speak of them as one, referring to them as 'the Christmas story'. But in reality they are very different from each other, and the habit of putting them together has tended to obscure the particular insights and characteristics of each of them. In this Study we shall examine more closely what it is that the author of Matthew's Gospel has to say about Jesus's birth, and try to expose the underlying points that he makes in his narrative. Scholars are generally agreed that he drew upon other sources for much of his information, but he has evidently adapted that material to suit his theological purposes. However, throughout this exploration we will need to bear in mind that the author was not concerned to produce a biographical record of what took place, but (like the other Gospel writers) wanted to create a document which would encourage acceptance of Jesus as the Son of God. We should therefore try to focus upon what he means, rather than attempt to reconstruct the actual physical events.

The family tree of Jesus

Matthew opens his Gospel by giving a conventional 'family tree' of Jesus. He begins with the figure of Abraham, having first highlighted Jesus's descent from David as a hint of what is to come later. The point of starting with Abraham is to affirm from the outset that Jesus is a true Hebrew, because no Jew of that time would have countenanced the possibility of a Messiah from outside Israel. The 'real' Messiah had to be Jewish. The line of descent is then pursued through the family of David, and up to the point in history when the Jews were taken away into exile by the Babylonians. The Exile had been a critical point in Jewish history, when many Jews entered into mixed marriages and thus put their racial purity in jeopardy; but Matthew then moves on from the Exile to the birth of Jesus, evidently seeing no break in the line of Jesus's descent, though something seems to go wrong when the list reaches the name of Joseph *(see Matthew 1:16)*. At that point he observes that Mary was the mother of Jesus, but shrinks back from acknowledging Joseph as his father – yet it is through Joseph, and not Mary, that the line of David proceeds. Thus the whole argument of lineage breaks down, because it is through the father, and not the mother, that Jewish family descent is always reckoned.

But there is an important ancient manuscript which offers a different version of verse 16, and it reads:

> '... *and Jacob was the father of Joseph, to whom the virgin Mary was betrothed; he was the father of Jesus who is called the Messiah.*'

There is some textual support for this version, but not as much as for the usual reading, which is why it does not appear in English translations. However, if it were to be allowed as the original text of Matthew 1:16 it would certainly solve the problem of the inconsistency of Matthew's argument: but it would also cause doctrinal problems because it would look as if the birth of Jesus was not particularly special, since it would not then be a virgin birth. It seems that the desire of the early Christian Church to defend the doctrine of Christ as 'Son of God' produced a strong reluctance to allow that Joseph was his physical father. However, Matthew's chief concern here is to assert the true Messiahship of Jesus, and he rounds off this part of his account by highlighting the pattern of events in a strange mathematically-symbolic way. He says that there were fourteen generations in each of the three periods from Abraham to David, from David to the Exile, and finally from the Exile to the birth of the Messiah. Scrupulous readers, however, will no doubt notice that in the third of these periods there are actually only thirteen generations mentioned. One name seems to be missing – perhaps an error on the author's part, or possibly a mistake by an early scribe, though it has been suggested that Matthew wanted to include Mary in the list as the fourteenth person.

The position of Joseph

The section of narrative which follows this family tree *(Matthew 1:18–25)* elaborates upon the issue of the involvement of Joseph in the birth of Jesus, and it explicitly denies that he was the biological father. In those days the betrothal of a man and a woman prior to their wedding (what we would refer to as their 'engagement') was treated as legally binding, so to discover that Mary was already pregnant before their actual marriage would indeed have been a cause of serious offence to Joseph. He is, however, reassured by an angelic visitor that the baby's birth is an act of God, and that he need not be ashamed. Apparently this is enough to satisfy Joseph, since the proposed separation does not then take place, and he remains betrothed to Mary, and marries her, but has no sexual relationship with her until after the birth of Jesus.

In Matthew 1:21 it is recorded that Joseph had the responsibility of naming the child. This was fully in accordance with Jewish custom, which gave the father the duty of choosing a name. That name was to be JESUS, which is the Greek version of the Hebrew name JOSHUA. This was, of course, also the name of the great figure of Hebrew antiquity, who succeeded Moses and led the Israelites into their promised land. Yet Matthew, in his desire to show that Jesus came in fulfilment of prophecy, then quotes from the book of Isaiah *(Isaiah 7:14)*, where it is said that a young woman will give birth to a child and will name him EMMANUEL ('God with us'). This is a somewhat contrived theological device on Matthew's part, since it is clear that in its original context that prophecy had nothing to do with a Messianic prediction. Nor did the word 'virgin' appear in that passage: the Hebrew word simply meant 'a young woman of marriageable age', and it was only a mistranslation in the Greek Version of the Old Testament which produced the word 'virgin'. But Matthew's fondness for finding prophetic support for his beliefs led him to grasp at this, despite the obvious fact that Christ was not actually named Emmanuel, but Jesus, in accordance with the instructions of Joseph.

Up to this point in the narrative, Joseph has had a significant place. But when we read through the rest of Matthew's Gospel we find that Joseph is hardly mentioned again. He drops out of the story of Jesus altogether, without explanation. His name occurs in Matthew 2:13–14, and again in 2:19, in the context of the secret flight into Egypt to escape the plotting of King Herod, but as far as Matthew is concerned that is the last we ever hear of him. Later Christian tradition has suggested that he died while Jesus was still quite young, though according to Luke's Gospel Joseph was still alive when Jesus was twelve years old *(see Luke 2:41–51)*, and is there quite openly referred to as his father.

The coming of the wise men

After the narrative of Christ's birth there follows the highly-imaginative story of the Wise Men who come 'from the East' to search for the newly-born king of the Jews. It is only Matthew's Gospel which contains this story, and scholars are generally agreed that Matthew received this tradition from another source. It never formed part of the early Christian Gospel message. But regardless of the source of this part of the narrative, Matthew adapts it to fit in with his theological plan, linking it with Old Testament history and prophecy. What he seems to be affirming is that when the Messiah was born it was not the Jewish leaders themselves who recognised or acknowledged his coming, but Gentiles. We are not told here how these mysterious figures came to know of Jesus's birth, though the general implication seems to be that it was through astrological methods. This may be the significance of the star which is said to guide them to the right place. The reference to the 'east' could perhaps point to Persia, where this kind of thinking was commonplace.

They bring with them an array of gifts. Three in particular are mentioned – gold, frankincense and myrrh, giving rise to the tradition that there were actually three wise men in all, though the narrative gives no such information. What the gifts represented is probably costliness, as befitted an important figure: attempts to interpret them as having to do with majesty, worship and death are no more than romantic speculation.

What Matthew then does is to link this tradition (which has all the marks of religious mythology) with the story of Moses in the Old Testament, depicting King Herod in the role of the cruel Pharaoh who wanted to kill all the Hebrew male children *(see Exodus 1:22ff)*. Jesus is said to have been taken into Egypt for safety – probably to give Matthew the opportunity to offer yet another Old Testament prophecy in support of Jesus's Messiahship – 'Out of Egypt I have called my son' *(Matthew 2:13–15, see also Hosea 11:1)*. But to give his story some historical continuity, Matthew then explains that when the threat from Herod was over (he provides no time scale here), Joseph was given divine instructions to take Mary and the child into Israel, where the family eventually settled in Nazareth. Even here, Matthew cannot resist yet another attempt to find a supporting Old Testament prophecy – but this time he fails, on two counts. He says that the prophets had predicted.

'he shall be called a Nazorean' (Matthew 2:23),

but there is in fact no such prophecy anywhere in the Old Testament. Nor did the word 'Nazorean' refer to someone from Nazareth, though clearly Matthew thought that it did, and the early Christian Church accepted his interpretation.

The religious value of Matthew's birth narrative

All down the centuries there have been disagreements about the historicity of this account of Jesus's birth. Opinions have varied, ranging from those who have tried to prove that there really was a star or planet which behaved oddly, to those who have dismissed the entire narrative as pious fiction. But from the point of view of the serious Christian interpreter, this story makes certain very significant points. First, it insists upon the continuity of Jesus's birth with the history of God's purposes as set out in the Old Testament. That is to say, the birth of Jesus was not a 'flash in the pan': it was the inevitable and proper outcome of God's on-going intentions for the salvation of humankind. It links the Old Testament and the New Testament inseparably together. Second, it affirms the direct involvement of God in Jesus's birth. This is what is signified in the account of his miraculous conception. Whether we take the story literally and insist that this was indeed a true (and therefore unique) virgin birth, or whether we prefer to see the birth as entirely normal and thereby preserve the tradition of Jesus's full humanity is, in the last resort, a question of personal religious belief.

POINTS FOR DISCUSSION

1. There are only two accounts in the entire New Testament which describe the events of Jesus's birth, and they are very different from one another. What might this imply as to its centrality in Christian belief?

2. Is there any contemporary value in insisting that Jesus was the expected Jewish Messiah? Or was Matthew's argument relevant only as a way of encouraging the Jews of his time to convert to Christianity?

3. Would Christian faith be damaged or enhanced by accepting that Joseph was the human father of Jesus? Could you give reasons for your opinion?

4. What is the religious value of the imagery and symbolism in Matthew's account of Christ's birth?

5. Why might Matthew want to say that it was the Gentiles, not Jesus's own people, who first recognised him as the Christ? Is this perhaps a parallel to the statement in John's Gospel that 'he came unto his own people, and his own people did not receive him' *(John 1:11)*? Does it

suggest that it is possible to be so familiar with the figure of Jesus that we fail to see him for what he really is?

6. How important is it for Christians that the Old Testament should be retained as the foundation for the New Testament revelation of Christ? Could we not now dispense with the Old Testament altogether?

5 | Luke's Birth Narrative

We now turn to the other Gospel which contains an account of the birth of Christ – the Gospel of Luke *(see Luke 1:26 to 2:52)*. In our previous Study we saw that Matthew's Gospel had a distinctly Jewish flavour to it, and that the author was concerned to demonstrate that Jesus was the expected Jewish Messiah, whose coming had been foretold by the prophets. But here in Luke's Gospel we have a very different approach. Scholars are generally agreed that Luke was not Jewish, but a Gentile, though he does display a close familiarity with Jewish ideas. The whole of his Gospel shows clear Gentile sympathies, and a much broader approach to the meaning of the coming of Christ. Whereas Matthew wanted to show that Christ was the fulfilment of Judaism, Luke wants to demonstrate the universal significance of the Christian message, which he sees as being addressed to the whole of humanity.

The preface to the birth narrative

Before dealing with the miraculous birth of Jesus, Luke makes reference to the figure of John the Baptist, whose birth, he says, was also an act of God. John's father was a priest by the name of Zechariah, and his mother (Elizabeth) was a member of another priestly family, descended from Aaron. Luke stresses the fact that Elizabeth was incapable of bearing children, and that in any case both she and her husband were getting on in years. Evidently Elizabeth's inability to bear a child had been something of a social disgrace *(see Luke 1:24–25)*, so the fact that she had conceived at last was even more significant: not only was she to have a baby – she was also to have her disgrace taken away. We are reminded here of other Old Testament figures to whom children were born in strange circumstances. In Genesis 21:1ff it is recorded that Sarah and Abraham had a child even though they were themselves very advanced in years, and in I Samuel 1:20ff it is said that Hannah gave birth to Samuel although 'the LORD had closed her womb' *(see I Samuel 1:4–6)*, and she too had been subjected to severe social criticism. The prophet Jeremiah sets this same theme into a somewhat different context when he describes the Israelite people as unloved outcasts who are to be blessed by God as a mark of his forgiving grace, and that they will once again bear children:

> 'Out of them shall come thanksgiving, and the sound of merrymakers. I will make them many, and they shall not be few; I will make them honoured, and they shall not be disdained. Their children shall be as of old ...'
> *(Jeremiah 30:19ff)*

So we are introduced by Luke to the idea of an impending birth which defies the laws of nature, and which symbolises a mighty forgiving act of God, as a kind of prelude or curtain-raiser to the coming of Christ himself. Just as Mary, the mother of Jesus, is later to be visited by an angel, so also the same thing happens to Zechariah *(Luke 1:11ff)*. This part of the story is very strongly reminiscent of a passage in Matthew's Gospel *(see Matthew 1:18–25)*, where an angel visits Joseph to reassure him, and some scholars suspect that the two traditions actually come from the same source, though we do not know what this was. Zechariah is warned that the coming baby (John) will possess the spirit and power of the Old Testament prophet Elijah *(Luke 1:17)*, who, according to Jewish tradition, was expected to return to earth as a herald of the coming of the Messiah, and to prepare people to receive him. So, in one short account, Luke contrives to emphasise not only the importance of the figure of John the Baptist, but also his subordinate position to that of Jesus.

The appearance of the angel Gabriel to both Zechariah *(Luke 1:11ff)* and Mary *(Luke 1:26ff)* gives the narrative a special kind of continuity, implying that the birth of John the Baptist and then the birth of Jesus Christ were part of the same divine event.

But it is interesting to note that this is the only place in Luke's writings where an angelic messenger is actually named: although angels figure in later incidents *(see Luke 2:9, Luke 22:43, Acts 5:19, Acts 10:3, Acts 12:7)*, they are not given names, and they do not engage in the kind of detailed conversations described in this particular story. In all those subsequent passages, what the angels have to say is confined strictly to the message they bring, or else they say nothing at all. Scholars have pointed out that it is only in the later parts of the Old Testament that angels are ever given names, and it has been suggested that this practice was brought back into Israelite religion from Babylonian customs picked up during the Exile. The name 'Gabriel' itself is obviously associated with the name of God, as the suffix 'el' indicates, and it could mean something like 'Man of God'.

The Annunciation

According to Luke, it was while Elizabeth was six months into her pregnancy that her cousin Mary also received an angelic visitation. At that point in time Mary was engaged to be married to Joseph – who once again, as in Matthew's Gospel, is carefully identified as being descended from David *(Luke 1:27)*. The message brought by Gabriel was that Mary would soon conceive and give birth to a son, and that she would call him by the name of Jesus. He would inherit the throne of David, and his kingdom would never come to an end. Mary is said to express great surprise at this announcement, and protests that she is still a virgin, but the angel comforts her with the news that the birth would not be the result of a human relationship, but will come about by the power of the Holy Spirit, thereby giving her a holy child. The notion of the Holy Spirit overshadowing or 'spreading his wings' over Mary is reminiscent of certain Old Testament passages *(such as Ruth 3:9 and Ezekiel 16:8)*, where it is suggestive of sexual intercourse. Just as Elizabeth, her cousin, has been miraculously granted a child in her old age, so also God is to work a miracle within Mary herself.

This particular narrative bears the marks of factual inconsistency. It is not clear why Mary should be surprised to learn that she will have a child, since she is already engaged to be married, and is still young enough to bear children. The prospect of having a baby at some point in the near future ought not, therefore, to have startled her, though the manner in which the delivery of the message took place certainly was very special. However, this inconsistency is not at all out of keeping with the tone of the entire birth narrative, since Luke is setting all of it in a framework of what has been called 'sacred surprise'. He seems to be trying to show that what happened was in the nature of a divine intervention, rather than (as in Matthew's Gospel) the climax of a long-drawn-out process. If Christ's birth was foreseen by the prophets of Judaism, it certainly came like a bolt from the blue to Gentiles.

The three songs

In these first two chapters of Luke's Gospel there appear three songs which deserve special consideration. The first is the **Magnificat** *(Luke 1:46–56)*, which is given that name because of its opening words in the Latin translation. It shows very close similarities to the song of Hannah *(see I Samuel 2:1ff)* in the Old Testament, and is essentially a song of praise and thanksgiving, which a few scholars of the late nineteenth century thought should have been placed on the lips of Elizabeth rather than of Mary. In Christian tradition this song has been adopted for use in the liturgy of worship, both in the western Church and in the Greek Church. Then there is a second song, attributed to Zechariah and occasioned by the birth of John the Baptist. This is commonly referred to as the **Benedictus** *(Luke 1:67–69)*, again because of its Latin beginning, and it takes the form of a prophecy in verse, linking John's birth with Messianic expectations and also declaring that his role will be that of preparing the way for the coming of the Lord. Here also, this passage has been drawn into Christian liturgies. The third song is known as the **Nunc Dimittis** *(see Luke 2:29–32)*, and is said to have been uttered by Simeon, a devout Jew who has the religious insight to recognise Jesus as the Jewish Messiah. He praises God that his prayers have been answered, and that he has been privileged to witness the arrival of the one who will not only bring glory to Israel but also revelation to the Gentile world. Ever since the fourth century AD this song has been included in both eastern and western Christian liturgies.

The birth of Jesus

Luke places the occasion of the birth of Jesus as coinciding with a census taken when Quirinius was the Syrian governor. Apparently this was not merely a local event, but was empire-wide *(see Luke 2:1, where it is said that 'all the world' was to be registered)*. This piece of information has caused a great deal of difficulty for scholars who have tried to identify the specific year of Christ's birth. The difficulty lies in the chronology itself. It is known from other sources that a census did indeed take place when Quirinius held office, and in Acts 5:37 Luke shows that he knew about this – but it was actually held in AD 6 to 7, when it provoked a revolt to which Luke referred in the above passage. It is, therefore, not easy to see why Luke should link the birth of Jesus to this particular census, especially as he also says that Jesus was born when Herod the Great was king of Judea *(see Luke 1:5)*, and we know, again from other very reliable sources, that Herod died in 4 BC. Numerous attempts have been made to explain this mysterious inconsistency, but none has been altogether satisfactory: it has been argued, for example, that Quirinius was not actually the Syrian governor at that point, but was still holding the lower rank of *legatus*, and that this therefore accounts for Luke's confusion over dates. Others have suggested that Luke was mistaken about the name of the governor, and yet others have claimed that there must have been another census to which Luke was really referring. One scholar went so far as to argue that Luke took his information from a source which had political interests, and which had deliberately tried to link the birth of Jesus with the rise of the Zealot movement. Whatever the truth may be, it seems that at present there is no obvious way of resolving this difficulty, and we have to settle for the fact that the precise date of Christ's birth is not known.

Like Matthew, Luke claims that Jesus was born in Bethlehem, but he adds that the birth took place in very humble – even menial – circumstances. Mary gave birth to her child in a stable, because all the inns were fully occupied, presumably by the many visitors who had also come to be registered. The notion of a humble birth fitted Luke's theology very well indeed, because all through his Gospel he was at pains to show that Christ came to bring good news to people in the lower ranks of society – the poor, the social outcasts, and to women (who in Jewish custom ranked lower than men, despite the attempts of later Jewish apologists to defend their social status by defining it as 'honourable').

Luke says nothing about wise men coming from the east. Instead, he describes shepherds in their fields at night, guarding their flocks; they (like Mary and Joseph) receive an angelic visitation, and they too are said to be afraid, in the sense that they are overpowered by religious awe. They are told that a child has been born in the city of David, who is the Jewish Messiah, and that the circumstances of his birth are in themselves a 'sign' by which he can be identified. In the light of what Luke has previously said, we can assume that the city of David is a reference to Bethlehem, though it should not be overlooked that this name was also given to the city of Jerusalem, which David had captured and made his own. The angel refers to Jesus as 'Saviour', and here Luke appears to be giving this word a meaning which went much deeper than that of a purely political leader.

The shepherds hurried to Bethlehem, where they found the child with Mary and Joseph. They spoke publicly about their strange experience and about what they had been told concerning the true nature of the newborn baby, but Mary (who, we can suppose, already knew about these predictions because of her own experience), simply kept the matter to herself *(see Luke 2:19)*. This theme of spreading the good news is a feature of Luke's writings, and he manages to introduce it even into the birth narrative – unlike Matthew, who never suggests that the wise men spoke publicly about what they had seen, but restricts himself to saying that they simply paid homage to the child.

In this narrative Joseph is openly mentioned as being present and as being Jesus's father. Possibly, though not certainly, there might be some significance in the fact that Mary's name precedes that of Joseph *(see Luke 2:16)*, but no embarrassment on this score is evident later in the narrative *(see Luke 2:33)* where Joseph is referred to as the father of the new baby. The two parents are said to be together for the ritual of circumcision and for the ceremony of purification in the Temple *(see Luke 2:21–24)*, and there is no hint that Joseph's presence was in any way subordinate to that of Mary as far as responsibility was concerned. Evidently he was taking on the full duties of a Jewish father.

Luke says, somewhat curiously, that Mary and Joseph were amazed at what was being said about Jesus *(Luke 2:33)*, and they are again astonished when, at the age of twelve, he was found in the Jerusalem Temple, showing a degree of religious understanding which went far beyond his years *(see Luke 2:41–51)*. It is difficult to see why they should be so surprised, since from the time of his birth, and indeed even before it, they had apparently been made aware that he was a very special child. Once again Luke tells us that 'Mary treasured all these things in her heart' *(Luke 2:31)*, implying that secretly she knew what his true nature was, so again it seems inconsistent to suggest that her child's behaviour took her by surprise. Some commentators have claimed that the reference may possibly be understood as an allusion to Genesis 37:11, where it is said that Jacob was secretly aware of the mysterious power of his son Joseph, but kept the matter to himself even though his other sons showed jealousy. However, if it is correct to say that Luke was a Gentile, and not a Jew, this kind of abstract Biblical interpretation is not really very likely.

The historicity of Luke's birth narrative

Are we to take Luke's account literally? When examining the birth narrative in Matthew's Gospel it became evident that mythological elements had been incorporated into the story, and here again we find the same characteristic. The frequent references to angelic visitations, and the constant predictions of the child's special nature, show that the actual facts of Jesus's birth have been overlaid with religious tradition and interpretation. This is not at all surprising: it is a feature of virtually all birth narratives in the ancient religions of the world. In Indian tradition, for example, the birth of Siddhartha Gautama (the Buddha) in the sixth century BC was said to have been attended by quite astonishing events, including the claim that he was conceived when his mother stepped in the footprint of a god. One eminent Buddhist writer has observed:

> *'Many miraculous tales have arisen concerning the birth of the child and his early development. Such tales seem to be one of the occupational hazards of religious leaders ...'*
> *(H. Saddhatissa, **The Buddha's Way**, Allen & Unwin 1971, pp. 19–20)*

But to suggest that Luke's narrative contains elements of religious interpretation, expressed in the form of mythology, should not in any way damage its value. In the last resort, all historical events are coloured by the evaluation and interpretation of the historian, and are passed down to posterity not merely as straight facts but as events which carry their own significance within themselves. What Luke and Matthew have done is to lay that significance open to full view, and to expose not only the fact of the birth of Christ but also its deeper meaning. When we turn to examine what the writer of the fourth Gospel has to say, we shall discover that he leaves out the 'facts' altogether, and opens up the inner meaning to full view.

POINTS FOR DISCUSSION

1. In what sense can it be said that the coming of Christ is of universal significance? Does it mean that all the other religions of the world have been rendered valueless?
2. Luke evidently wants to show Christ's birth as a divine intervention into human affairs. Does this conflict with Matthew's idea that it was all part of God's eternal plan, known to the prophets from the beginning?
3. In the light of what is said about Mary in both of the birth narratives, has the Roman Catholic Church been right to venerate her in the way that it does? Or does she play a relatively unimportant role as the mother of Jesus?
4. Is there any link between Luke's emphasis upon miraculous births and his later ideas concerning Christ's resurrection from the dead, when 'life' came out of a seemingly impossible situation?
5. How are we to understand 'angels' in our modern world? Do they have any genuine existence today, and if so, in what form?
6. Does it matter that we cannot discover the precise date of Christ's birth?
7. How can it be said today that the Gospel of Christ is addressed to the poor? Who, exactly, *are* the poor?

6 | The Word Became Flesh

In this Study we are to look at the incarnation as seen by the author of the fourth Gospel. We shall be referring to him, following ancient tradition, as 'John', though that should not be taken as an acceptance that he is to be identified as John the Apostle. The weight of evidence strongly suggests that he was not: but, whoever he was, his Gospel reveals the fact that he was a very subtle thinker, with a grasp not only of theological issues but also of philosophical concepts.

The purpose of John's gospel

Like the Gospel of Mark, this book does not provide us with a birth narrative as such. Indeed, it appears to cast some doubt even upon the tradition that Jesus was born in Bethlehem:

> 'But some asked, 'Surely the Messiah does not come from Galilee, does he? Has not the scripture said that the Messiah is descended from David and comes from Bethlehem, the village where David lived? (John 7:41–42)

But John's purpose was not to engage in arguments about whether Jesus came from Nazareth or from Bethlehem: his main concern was to show that Jesus came from God, and indeed this is the fundamental theme of the entire Gospel. It is as if he was saying that the question of the historical events surrounding Jesus's birth is largely irrelevant when set against the much more profound question of his true nature as Son of God. His aim is to probe into the mystery of the relationship between Jesus and God, and to lay bare his personal conviction that it is only through acceptance of Jesus's true nature that 'eternal life' becomes available:

> *'These things are written so that you may come to believe that Jesus is the Messiah, the Son of God, and that through believing you may have life in his name'. (John 20:31)*

It seems likely that John knew at least something of the work of the writers of the first three (Synoptic) Gospels, because he is probably alluding to them in an oblique kind of way in his opening verses *(1:1–18, commonly referred to as the Prologue)*, or at least he knew of a similar tradition to that which the Synoptic writers represented. He repeats the Synoptic tradition concerning John the Baptist *(see John 1:6–9, 15)*, but he then moves on to expand his message further – possibly because he felt that the Synoptic accounts were not altogether satisfactory. Certainly he would have been unhappy with Mark's way of putting things: Mark suggests that Jesus became Son of God, not at his birth but at the time of his baptism in the river Jordan, in a passage that could very easily encourage belief that Jesus was somehow 'adopted' by God *(see Mark 1:9–11)*. The Gospels of Matthew and Luke could also have appeared to be too much inclined towards pagan mythology in their assertions about angels, astrological signs and miraculous births. John evidently wanted to retain a firm grip upon the principle that a true incarnation had taken place, but at the same time he wanted to present that truth in a more telling way. He also wanted to make it plain that Jesus did not become divine at some point during his earthly life, but was indeed so from the very beginning.

There is also good reason to believe that John was aware of a teaching, current in his own day, which came out of a special fashion of thinking generally referred to as Gnosticism. In particular, there was a view about Jesus which asserted that he was not a true human being at all, but an apparition. It was being said that he was not a real man, but only went through the motions of living a normal human life in order to accommodate himself to his associates. This view, known as **Docetism** (from a Greek word meaning 'to appear or to seem to be'), arose out of the difficulty of holding together Christ's human and divine natures. It was said that if he was God, then he could not be a man, since God is pure spirit, while human beings are made of imperfect flesh and blood. John was astute enough to appreciate that such a doctrine, if it were allowed to spread, would destroy the whole point of the Gospel, because it would effectively deny the truth of the incarnation. It would, of course, also destroy the claim that Jesus suffered and died a human death on the Cross, and there could then be no true resurrection. The heresy was highly dangerous. So, at the very beginning of his Gospel, John lays down the basic principle that 'the Word' (LOGOS) actually became real flesh and blood *(John 1:14)*, and lived a human life among other human beings. It is not possible here to embark upon a thorough examination of what the 'Logos' meant for John, but we can say that in a sense it represents the eternal creative purpose of God, by which (or whom) everything comes into being. In the book of Genesis it is said that God created the universe by speaking it into existence *(see Genesis 1:1ff)*: his utterance is also his deed. As one New Testament scholar put it in his commentary on John's Gospel:

> *'... John seeks to convey to his readers of every age that what took place as divine action in the life of Jesus Christ was not some 'afterthought' of God, but the true embodiment in a personal historical life of the whole purpose of God, and of all the meaning of the universe.'* (John Marsh, **Saint John**, Pelican Commentary 1968, p. 97)

The 'Virgin Birth' in John's gospel

We have observed that there is no birth narrative as such in John's Gospel, but there is certainly a careful exploration of the idea of a virgin birth. John does not express it in the same way as did Matthew and Luke, but in the Prologue to his book he makes this remarkable statement:

> *'... to all who received him, who believed in his name, he gave power to become children of God, who were born, not of blood or of the will of the flesh or of the will of man, but of God'.* (John 1:12–13)

His point is that those who, by faith, acknowledge and receive Christ, enjoy a 'new birth' which is not conceived by any human agency or power but is given wholly by the grace of God. In short, every Christian is the product of a 'virgin birth', and Jesus himself led the way by virtue of his own nature. Here we catch distinct echoes of St Paul's teaching about Christians being 'justified by faith alone' *(see, for example, Romans 8:12–14)*.

The same idea comes through again in John's account of the conversation between Jesus and Nicodemus *(see John 3:1ff)*. Nicodemus, a Pharisaic Jew, talks secretly with Christ and shows strong sympathies with what he is doing. Jesus replies to the effect that sympathies are not enough: there must be a 'new birth', which can come about only by an act of God, and not through any 'fleshly' means. Once more we see John affirming the principle of a Divine intervention or a new creation.

John's view of Jesus as Son of God

In the main body of his Gospel, John goes on to develop his claim that Jesus and God are one. He does it in several ways. He illustrates it by references to the works of Jesus, carried out during the course of his ministry – works which are obviously meant to be understood as the works of God himself *(see, for example, John 2:1–11, John 5:1–18, and John 9:1–41)*. This is very much in line with the approach of the other three Gospel writers. But John departs from the Synoptic tradition altogether when he pictures Jesus engaging in long and detailed discussions on the subject of his own nature. Whereas in the Synoptic Gospels it is commonly the ordinary people who watch Jesus at work and then proclaim their recognition of who he is, in the fourth Gospel it is Jesus himself who expounds upon his close relationship with God, in language that is very reminiscent of philosophical theology.

In chapter 5 of John's Gospel the writer presents Jesus as teaching directly about his own nature and status. Christ can do nothing on his own, but only what the Father does *(John 5:19)*.

Just as the Father gives life at creation, so also the Son gives new life *(John 5:21)*. The Son carries out the divine work of judgment *(John 5:22 and 5:27)*. Anyone who refuses to honour the Son is also refusing to honour the Father *(John 5:23)*.

In chapter 6 the question of Jesus's human parentage is openly faced:

> *'Then the Jews began to complain about him because he said, "I am the bread that came down from heaven." They were saying, "Is not this Jesus, the son of Joseph, whose father and mother we know? How can he now say, "I have come down from heaven"?' (John 6:41–42)*

It should be noted that in this passage John makes no attempt to deny that Joseph was the father of Jesus. That is not his intention, and we may be fully justified in thinking that John could accept Jesus's human parentage without feeling that it contradicted his relationship with God as his Father.

In chapter 8 Jesus is reported to claim that he is the light of the world *(John 8:12ff)*, and that if his critics really knew him they would also know God *(John 8:19)*. But without doubt the most direct and even the most audacious statements are found in chapter 14, where Jesus holds a conversation with the two disciples Thomas and Philip, and makes some astounding claims about his own person:

> *'If you know me, you will know my Father also. From now on you do know him and have seen him.' (John 14:7)*

> *'Whoever has seen me has seen the Father. How can you say "Show us the Father"? Do you not believe that I am in the Father and the Father is in me?' (John 14:9–10)*

It is also in a further conversation with Thomas, this time after the resurrection, that Jesus invites the doubting disciple to reach out his hand and touch him, whereupon Thomas responds with the words 'My Lord and my God!' *(see John 20:28)*.

To feel the force of these and many other such statements which John places on the lips of Jesus it is necessary to read through the whole of this Gospel: but enough has been said here to illustrate the way in which the author picks his way through the paradox of the incarnation. He balances the full and true humanity of Jesus with his absolute conviction that, in this man, God is genuinely and fully 'with us'. Yet he manages to do it without any direct reference to the events of Jesus's birth, because for him the incarnation was not so much a physical arrival on earth as a spiritual experience of a divinely-initiated reality.

The Holy Spirit in the Fourth Gospel

In the Gospels of Matthew and Luke, the Holy Spirit is said to have been the agent of God in the act of Jesus's conception. Matthew sets this teaching in the context of the angel's reassurances to Joseph:

'Joseph, son of David, do not be afraid to take Mary as your wife, for the child conceived in her is from the Holy Spirit.' (Matthew 1:20),

and Luke embodies the same idea in Mary's encounter with the angel Gabriel:

'The angel said to her, "The Holy Spirit will come upon you, and the power of the Most High will overshadow you; therefore the child to be born will be holy ..." ' (Luke 1:35)

John, however, approaches this rather differently. Like the Synoptic writers, he affirms that all those who receive Christ and thereby enjoy a new birth must be born 'of the Spirit' *(see John 3:1–8)*, but later in his Gospel he gives the Holy Spirit an extended role. He records Jesus as telling his disciples that, after he has left them, the Holy Spirit will come from the Father, to teach them everything and to keep them mindful of all that Jesus himself has taught them *(John 14:25–26 and 15:26)*. Here we have the raw material which was later to be drawn into the formulation of the Christian doctrine of the Trinity. It is as if the Spirit which was the creative force or power in the birth of Jesus is also active in the new birth of every believing Christian, and just as the Spirit sustained Christ, so also that sustaining and empowering role is continued in those who make up the church.

POINTS FOR DISCUSSION

1. The author of the Fourth Gospel offers his interpretation of the incarnation of God in Christ, rather than an account of the events surrounding Jesus's birth. Does this mean that the actual events on their own are unimportant? At Christmas, do Christians celebrate the events, or do they celebrate what those events mean? Or are the two inseparable?

2. What does John mean when he says that all those who receive Christ are 'born, not of blood or of the will of the flesh or of the will of man, but of God' (John 1:13)? Is he talking about a different kind of 'virgin birth'?

3. In what sense can it be said today that a Christian must experience a new birth? Is this the same thing as a 'conversion experience'? Is it what the Christmas hymn means when it invites Christ to 'be born in us today'?

4. *'True God of true God, Light of Light eternal,*
   Lo, he abhors not the virgin's womb;
   Son of the Father, begotten, not created...'
   Does the significance of these words become any clearer after reading the Gospel of John?

5. What do you understand by John's statement that the Word became flesh? What sort of 'word' is he referring to?

6. It has often been said that the Christ of the Fourth Gospel is very different from the Christ pictured in the first three Gospels. Do you agree?

7 | The Incarnation in Paul's Theology

We have looked at the ways in which the birth of Jesus is presented in the Gospels, and now we turn to look at what St Paul had to say on this matter. It is one of the most notable features of Paul's letters that he appears to show little or no interest at all in the earthly life of Jesus. He makes hardly any direct mention of his teachings, or of his miracles, and indeed we are hard pressed to find anything that can be attributed to the lips of Jesus himself. Here and there we find fleeting allusions, but virtually nothing that can be traced directly back to the traditions about Christ's ministry. When he does speak of Jesus in a personal way, it is always the risen Lord who fills his mind. He seems to have no wish to make reference to the facts of Christ's earthly ministry. As one scholar has put it,

> *'There is absolutely nothing to suggest that it ever occurred to Paul to tell the story of Jesus of Nazareth in, for example, a Gospel, as was done decades later, first by Mark and then by others ...'.*
> *(Gunther Bornkamm, **Paul**, Hodder and Stoughton 1971, p.xxi)*

The reason for this is not hard to discover. Paul was a Christian missionary, and the most important aspect of his work was that of preaching the Gospel. The Gospel, for him, was essentially the good news of what Christ's death and resurrection had achieved. His aim was always that of showing how faith in Christ could bring the 'sinner' into a new relationship with God, and this meant that he wanted to concentrate not upon what Jesus said or did during his ministry, but upon what his life, death and resurrection had made possible. It is not the earthly Jesus, but the risen and glorified Christ who dominates Paul's thought. This may well be the meaning of an enigmatic passage in one of Paul's letters:

> '*From now on, therefore, we regard no-one from a human point of view; even though we once knew Christ from a human point of view, we know him no longer in that way ...*'.
> *(2 Corinthians 5:16)*

But it almost goes without saying that Paul was familiar with the current Christian traditions about Jesus. In his first letter to the Corinthians he mentions that he had received these traditions and had passed them on:

> '*For I handed on to you as of first importance what I in turn had received: that Christ died for our sins in accordance with the scriptures, and that he was buried, and that he was raised on the third day in accordance with the scriptures, and that he appeared to Cephas (Peter), then to the twelve. Then he appeared to more than five hundred brothers and sisters at one time, most of whom are still alive, though some have died. Then he appeared to James, then to all the apostles. Last of all, as to one untimely born, he appeared also to me ...*' *(1 Corinthians 15:3ff)*

Evidently his own personal experience of Jesus was post-resurrection: he shows no sign of ever having met or even seen Jesus during the time of the Galilean ministry, though he was certainly his contemporary. However, all this should not be taken to imply that Paul did not take the earthly life of Jesus seriously, or that he regarded his humanity as irrelevant to the Gospel of the risen Lord. In his letter to the Christians in Rome, he wrote:

> '*For God has done what the law, weakened by the flesh, could not do: by sending his own Son in the likeness of sinful flesh, and to deal with sin, he condemned sin in the flesh ...*'
> *(Romans 8:3)*

In this single sentence he affirms the full humanity of Jesus, with all that it implies. It is of the essence of Paul's entire theology that Jesus shared completely in the human condition, because his central theme is that of the way in which God has bridged the gap between himself and his creation. Paul writes of God 'reconciling' the world to himself *(see 2 Corinthians 5:19)*, that is, of bringing humanity and deity together as he did in the first act of creation, where mankind was made 'in God's image'. Christ was the 'new Adam', or new humanity, succeeding through obedience where the old Adam had gone wrong by disobedience. It would therefore be quite wrong to think that Paul had no 'theology of incarnation', but had replaced it with a pure 'theology of resurrection'.

Although Paul does not make mention of the birth of Jesus, he does include in his letters two very remarkable statements which have a direct bearing upon it. One is to be found in his letter to the Philippians *(Philippians 2:5–11)*, and the other in his correspondence with the Colossians *(Colossians 1:15–20 and 2:9)*. Both of them have very significant things to say about Christ's divine and human nature, and we can look at each of them in turn.

The 'Hymn to Christ'

The letter to the Philippians is one of the so-called Captivity Epistles, and is almost unanimously accepted by scholars as a genuine letter by Paul. Most of it is written in very personal terms, to a congregation which he evidently knew well, and of which he was very fond. But in the second chapter there occurs a passage which is in the form of a hymn (sometimes referred to as the Christological hymn), and it contains some of the most profound statements about Christ's nature to be found in the whole of the New Testament. There is a tendency among modern scholars to treat this hymn, not as Paul's own composition, but as having been taken over by him from some unknown Christian source: however, since by including it in his letter he obviously approved of what it says, we can accept it as reflecting his own thoughts.

Christ is described as being 'in the form of God', but (unlike the first Adam in the Genesis story) he did not try to elevate himself, or use his true nature for self-aggrandisement. Instead, he emptied himself and took the form of a slave. He was born in human likeness, and the measure of his obedience took him to the Cross, where he died. For this, he was exalted (or raised up) by God, and given 'the name that is above every name', so that everyone should regard him as Lord.

This statement is so full of important theological concepts that it is impossible to do full justice to it here. However, we can note that it implies that Jesus, though truly 'of God', somehow renounced his divinity and accepted the limitations of being fully human, even to the extent of accepting death itself. The Greek word which has been translated as 'emptying himself' *(kenosis)* has been the subject of a great deal of theological debate, and many different interpretations have been offered. Some scholars have understood it as meaning that Christ stripped himself of his divine nature in order to enter fully into human life, while others have said that he retained that nature but chose not to take advantage of it *(compare this with the story of his temptations in Matthew 4:1ff and Luke 4:1ff)*. The notion of his 'humility', or readiness to accept the human condition, is strongly reminiscent of the ideas contained in the Gospel of Luke, where Jesus is said to have been born in a humble environment. What is of special importance here is the way in which the incarnation is directly tied up with the crucifixion and resurrection of Christ.

Christ as the 'Image of God'

In the letter to the Colossians there is another significant statement about Christ's divine nature. Again, this letter has been widely acknowledged as a genuine work by Paul, written when he was in prison. In the opening chapter *(Colossians 1:15–20)*, and again briefly in a subsequent passage *(Colossians 2:9)*, Paul describes Jesus as embodying the fullness of God within himself. Once more we encounter the parallel with Adam, when Paul says that Jesus is the 'image of the invisible God' and the 'firstborn of all creation' *(Colossians 1:15)*. But Paul goes much further: he places Christ not merely within the created order but actually prior to it – he is 'before all things', and holds everything together *(Colossians 1:17)*. He is the firstborn from the dead and therefore has first place in everything. The implication of this is that Christ existed prior to his incarnation, and this pre-existence enabled him to embody the full extent of God's divine nature.

What is of special importance in Paul's thinking is that Christ's nature is inextricably bound up with his work of reconciling humanity with God. For Paul, that coming together was possible only if Jesus embodied within himself the full natures of both God and mankind. If Jesus had been less than human he could not have brought man to God: and if he had been less than God he could not have brought the Godhead into human affairs. So a full incarnation was essential, and it is in this sense that Paul treats the human life of Jesus so seriously. Unlike the Gospel writers, however, he does not present that human life in the framework of the historical Jesus, but in the context of Christ's completed work of living, dying and rising.

The Church as the Body of Christ

But before we leave Paul's teachings we must note a further element in his thinking which is of direct relevance to the birth of Christ, and that has to do with his view of the Christian Church as a kind of extension of the incarnation. Paul believed that the risen life of Christ has been made available to all, through faith. Those who acknowledge Christ in this manner are brought into fellowship with him through baptism *(see Romans 6:1ff)*. By being united with Christ through his death, the Christian is also united with Christ's resurrection, being made 'alive to God' *(Romans 6:11)*. Christians thus corporately make up the risen body of Christ, and their diversity is harmonised in the unity of that body *(see 1 Corinthians 12:4ff)*. What holds them together is the spirit of Christian love, which, like God himself, is eternal. It never ends *(see 1 Corinthians 13:8)*. It is the task of the Church to continue the earthly work of Christ, imitating him and feeding upon him. Christians must constantly test themselves to ensure that they are living in that faith, and to remind themselves that Christ is within them *(see 2 Corinthians 13:5)*. Just as it was the Spirit of God which was constantly empowering Christ, so also that same Spirit empowers the Body of Christ. As he was able to bear suffering, so must the members of his Body, knowing that beyond death there is resurrection. In all their afflictions they have the consolation of Christ *(see 2 Corinthians 1:3ff)*. As Jesus's humanity veiled his true nature as the embodiment of God, so it is with the Church; it does not present itself to the world as a mere human organisation, but rather it proclaims Christ, even though this truth is hidden in the earthly appearance of the human fellowship *(see 2 Corinthians 4:5–7)*.

In Paul's thinking, the Body of Christ (the Church) is, of course, his resurrected body. It is the post-resurrection incarnation. Nowhere does Paul ever suggest that the Church is perfect, because it is made up of human beings who are always subject to human weaknesses. Indeed, his correspondence with the Corinthian congregation illustrates only too clearly what those weaknesses are. Nevertheless, he is confident that it possesses the power to become what it ought to be. He can plead with the Colossians, for example, to 'seek the things that are above' *(see Colossians 3:1ff)*, because he is sure that they already possess the life of Christ and must constantly work to expose it. Their task is to bring their humanity into line with the Spirit that already dwells within them.

POINTS FOR DISCUSSION

1. In the light of Paul's presentation of Jesus as the new Adam, ought we to regard Jesus as 'a man' or as 'Man'?
2. How would you interpret the Christological hymn in Philippians 2:5–11? In particular, do you think that being 'in the form of God' means the same as 'being God', or that being 'in human likeness' means 'being fully human'?

3. If Christ 'emptied himself' of his divine nature during his time on earth, are we to conclude that throughout his ministry he was no longer God?
4. How could the fullness of God be embodied in a single human person?
5. What do you understand to be the nature of Christ's 'reconciling' work? How, if at all, is it linked with his birth?
6. Is it proper to think of the Church as a genuine extension of the incarnation? Do the obvious divisions and imperfections in the Christian Church destroy that idea?

8 The Celebration of Christmas

The date of Christmas

In this final Advent Study we shall look at the Christian celebration of the birth of Christ, in the light of what we have seen in the previous discussions, and at some of the customs which have found their way into the Christmas season. We can begin by noting that although Easter was celebrated from the very earliest times, it took much longer for Christmas to become an established festival. One of the first difficulties to be resolved was that of reaching agreement about the actual date of Christ's birth: no definite record of the event had been preserved, and even the year – let alone the precise day – was a matter of dispute. As we have observed, the Gospel of Luke shows some inconsistency, linking the birth with the occasion of a census under the Roman governor of Syria, Quirinius, but also saying that it took place when Herod the Great was king of Judaea, and these dates do not coincide.

As far as establishing the precise day was concerned, the absence of any clear evidence resulted in a great deal of speculation and guesswork – some of it very obscure indeed. In the early third century the Athenian theologian Clement of Alexandria (later to become St Clement) suggested that May 20th was the most likely date, but this proposal never received wide approval. Another suggestion was January 6th, and some Churches accepted this date – such as the Church of Jerusalem, which observed Christmas on that day until 549 AD. The Armenian Church, which, as its name implies, originated in Armenia but is today found in several countries (including England), still celebrates Christmas on January 6th, which is the date for celebrating Epiphany throughout the western Churches. The date appears to have some connection with a pagan water festival, which was held in Alexandria and linked with the winter solstice. Evidently the occasion of the birth of Jesus was at that time being very closely associated with the supposed date of his baptism by John in the river Jordan.

It was not until the year 336 that we find clear evidence of Christmas being celebrated on December 25th, and that date was almost certainly chosen deliberately to rival the Roman feast known as **Natalis Solis Invicti**, or the 'Birth of the Invincible Sun', and not because there was any evidence that it really was the day of Christ's birth. It may also have been associated with an ancient belief that the world was created at the vernal equinox (March 25th), and this date was possibly regarded as the day of Jesus's conception, with his birth taking place nine months later. Further evidence of the observance of Christmas on December 25th is found in an oration delivered by Gregory of Nazianzus in January 381, when he mentioned that the celebration of Christmas had been recently observed in Constantinople, and he describes how it had been marked by symbolically following the star, worshipping with the wise men, being bathed in light like the shepherds, gloryifing God along with the angels, taking Christ in their arms like Simeon, and confessing him as Lord like Anna the prophetess.

The doctrinal importance of Christmas

So the precise history of the inauguration of the Christmas festival remains something of a mystery, but it is certain that the main reason why Christians began so seriously to celebrate the birth of Jesus at all was that during the fourth and fifth centuries there were continuing discussions and controversies about his true nature, as the Church gradually worked out its formal doctrines with greater clarity. These debates, generally referred to as 'Christological' arguments, centred upon the issue to which our earlier Studies drew attention, namely, that of whether or not Jesus was a true human being, and, if he was, how he could also possess a divine nature. The problem of trying to balance his divinity with his humanity drove Christian theologians back to reconsider his birth in the light of his death and resurrection.

If he was truly God, then did this mean that he shared in God's eternal nature, having existed from the beginning'? If the end of his earthly life had been so significant, was the beginning of his life also meaningful? If he now enjoyed a new and glorified life after his resurrection, had he enjoyed an existence prior to his birth? Some of these matters had been touched upon in the New Testament documents, as we have already seen, but now they became increasingly important for the development of Christian theology and doctrine.

Christmas and Easter

Since it was the early Church's reflections upon the meaning of the death of Jesus which sent them back to reconsider his birth, it follows that if we are to understand the meaning of the incarnation we can do so only in the light of the resurrection. Christmas is largely unintelligible when totally separated from Easter: indeed, it becomes little more than a birthday celebration. Without Easter there is nothing particularly special about Jesus's birth. If we look carefully at the Christmas narratives in the Gospels of Matthew and Luke we see that they quite explicitly link his birth with his saving mission. Matthew describes the message which the angel delivered to Joseph after it had been found that Mary was pregnant:

> *'She will bear a son, and you are to name him Jesus, for he will save his people from their sins.' (Matthew 1:21)*

Luke writes about the angel Gabriel appearing to Mary and telling her that the child who is to be conceived in her womb

> *'... will be great, and will be called the Son of the Most High, and the Lord God will give to him the throne of his ancestor David. He will reign over the house of Jacob forever, and of his kingdom there will be no end.' (Luke 1:30ff)*

This is clearly Messianic language, in which the birth of the child is quite deliberately seen in terms of his future saving mission. He is important, not because of his birth alone, but because of the purpose behind that birth. The **Magnificat** (Luke 1:46ff) again affirms the future work of the coming child, and the message of the angels to the shepherds is that

> *'to you is born this day in the city of David a Saviour, who is the Messiah, the Lord'. (Luke 2:11)*

Always it is the anticipation of what is still to come that undergirds the excitement of what has happened. The birth of Christ and his saving work go together.

Advent and Christmas hymns

It is a useful exercise during the Advent season to examine some of the traditional hymns and carols which are sung at this time, to see which of them make this explicit link between the birth of Jesus and his death and resurrection, and which do not. Some do it very fully and very openly:

> *'Once there came to earth*
> *A child of lowly birth;*
> *Far from home the tiny stranger*
> *Lay contented in a manger,*
> *Jesus came to earth.*
>
> *'Then himself he gave,*
> *All the world to save:*
> *Sin and strife and hatred slew Him,*
> *Only those who loved him knew Him,*
> *Jesus strong to save!'*
>
> (A. Dorothy Angus)
>
> *'Then let us all with one accord*
> *Sing praises to our heavenly Lord,*
> *That hath made heaven and earth of nought,*
> *And with his blood mankind hath bought'*
>
> (Traditional)

Others lapse into an almost cloying sentimentality, in which the humanity of Jesus is swamped by pious attempts to picture his goodness, and no reference is made to his impending suffering and death:

> *'The cattle are lowing, the baby awakes,*
> *But little Lord Jesus no crying He makes ...*
>
> *(Anonymous)*

Yet others see Christ's birth in the context of highly sophisticated Christological formulae:

> *'True God of true God,*
> *Light of light eternal,*
> *Lo, He abhors not the virgin's womb;*
> *Son of the Father,*
> *Begotten, not created,*
> *O come, let us adore him, Christ the Lord.'*
>
> *(18th century Latin, translated by Frederick Oakeley)*

Study groups are invited to explore as many of these Christmas hymns as possible, and to analyse their contents in terms of what they have to say about the meaning of Christ's birth.

Christmas customs

Because Christmas festivities have a variety of origins it is not at all surprising to find that they have become very confused down the years. Many customs have crept in as a result of the coincidence of the Nativity and the numerous pagan midwinter observances that took place at about the same time of year. In Roman times the **Saturnalia** was the occasion of great merry-making and exchanging of gifts, and the latter custom was later mixed up with a similar practice associated with the Christian feast of **St Nicholas**, the patron saint of children, sea-travellers, and of the Russian people. The other Roman feast which we have already mentioned (the **Natalis Solis Invicti**) gave Christmas a very evident solar background associated with the beginning of the Roman New Year, when homes were decorated with greenery and bright lights. To all this were added further ingredients from several different cultures: **Yuletide** came from a Teutonic source and was probably connected with a Scandinavian feast to mark the change of the year. The word itself has something to do with 'clamour', which hints at the revelries that might have gone on. There was singing, dancing, and eating in abundance. The fact that Yuletide came at the same time of the year as Christmas inevitably brought the celebrations together, though strictly speaking they are quite unrelated.

The use of evergreens, as represented by the Christmas tree, probably originated from the eighth century, when St Boniface completed his work of converting Germany to the Christian religion, and dedicated the fir tree to the infant Jesus to replace the traditional oak, which was associated with the god Odin. It was from Germany that the custom of placing a tree in the family home was imported into England, largely through the influence of Queen Victoria's husband, Prince Albert. The figure of Father Christmas – a character in medieval street-plays and a symbol of excessive eating and drinking, became confused with that of Santa Claus (St Nicholas).

It is not possible here to elaborate upon the extraordinary way in which the Christian celebration of Christmas has become commercialised: but it is worth observing that during the time of Oliver Cromwell in England, it was made illegal to celebrate Christ's birth at all, precisely because the Puritans objected to the way in which it had encouraged bad practices, and for similar reasons Christmas was also suppressed for a time in the United States of America. With almost every successive year it is possible to see additional customs finding their way into the Christmas season, many of them coming from the European continent, and the original significance of the festival gradually becomes more and more obscured in popular perception. What began as a sophisticated and theologically subtle celebration has been turned into a festival aimed at children and the family, and it remains to be seen whether it will even disappear altogether.

POINTS FOR DISCUSSION

1. Oliver Cromwell banned the celebration of Christmas because he felt that it had lost its religious significance. Was he right to do this? Would any useful purpose be served if the Christian Church dissociated itself from the commercialised festivities of the present day?

2. When Christians sing hymns inviting the Messiah to come (for example, in the Advent hymn *'O come, O come Emmanuel'*), what exactly do they envisage happening?

3. Is there any harm in thinking of Christmas as being primarily a festival for children? What are we to make of those contemporary greetings cards which depict the Nativity in childish images (baby donkeys, small children dressed up as Mary and Joseph, etc.)? Is it true that Christmas loses its 'magic' when people grow up?

4. Has the custom of exchanging gifts at Christmas got out of hand? Does it still have any religious significance?

5. How could Christ be 'born in us today'?

6. What do you understand to be the meaning of the Christian teaching that Christ will one day return to earth at the 'Parousia' ('Second Coming')?

LENTEN STUDIES

1 Corporate Humanity

Adam as 'Everyman'

In the two creation stories contained in the book of Genesis *(Genesis 1:1–2:4a and 2:4bff)* the Hebrew word translated as 'man' is **Adam**. In subsequent Christian tradition the word has commonly been employed as if it were a name, but this is not strictly the case: it actually signifies the entire human race. Adam is 'everyman'. In the second (and older) of the two narratives, what happens to this one man is meant to be understood as happening to everyone, at all times and in all places. The narrative describes how Adam disobeyed God's law, was discovered, and was condemned to be cast out of the garden and forced to engage in arduous labour. In a magnificent piece of ancient poetry, he is told:

> *'By the sweat of your face you shall eat bread until you return to the ground, for out of it you were taken; you are dust, and to dust you shall return.' (Genesis 3:19)*

This is a careful and perceptive analysis of the whole human condition, summing up the contradiction of mankind's existence: there are times when people feel at home in the world, and there are other times when they feel alienated from it and deeply uncomfortable within it. Things are not as they should be, and this is true of the whole human race.

The narrative has been preserved within the body of scriptural literature which Jews have labelled **Torah**, or 'Law', despite the fact that superficially it has the appearance of history. It is not factual history at all in the modern sense, but religious myth, and its purpose was to preserve and pass on the spiritual insights of the past for the benefit of subsequent generations, concerning why people are as they are. It is a sensitively-drawn picture of the human condition, set in the context of human life and behaviour. It is told as if it was a single event which took place within time, but it is meant to be seen as timeless. The story constitutes religious guidance, which is what the word 'Torah' actually means. As the narrative proceeds, it sets out more specific illustrations of how human disobedience of God's directives will always and inevitably lead to punishment. It is 'law-in-action', making the point that although mankind has been given freedom to enjoy the world and to make choices, it is always freedom within limits set by God, and when that freedom is abused, God's wrath must follow. What is important for our present purposes is for us to note how the whole human race is here 'lumped together' and represented as if it were a single entity. Adam is portrayed as one man, but at the same time he is Everyman. Even his wife, Eve, is actually a part of him, because she is said to have been formed out of one of his ribs *(Genesis 2:21ff)*, and together they are 'one flesh'. This is not merely a convention of speech: it is one of the most important characteristics of the Biblical literature.

As the Old Testament literature unfolds and becomes more complex, it follows the conventions of referring to individual and distinct historical personalities, but this important concept of 'corporate humanity' is never very far beneath the surface. Over and over again, the Hebrew community ('the people of God') appears as a single individual, such as, for example, in the book of the prophet Hosea, where the name 'Israel' is used as the name of a child, but is then referred to as a whole nation:

> *'When Israel was a child, I loved him, and out of Egypt I called my son. The more I called them, the more they went from me ...' (Hosea 11:1–2)*

The great Emil Brunner, sometime Professor of Theology in the University of Zurich, wrote:

> *'This is the Biblical idea of man, that God, since He creates me as responsible, creates me in and for community with others. The isolated individual is an abstraction, conceived by*

> *the reason which has been severed from the Word of God ... I am not man at all apart from others ... Robinson Crusoe's whole longing was to mingle once again with human beings, in order to become a human being once more.'* (Emil Brunner, **Man in Revolt**, *Lutterworth Press, Third impression 1947, p.140)*

The Old Testament narrative affirms that in Adam, all humanity has sinned – but it does not explain how. It was later Christianity which attempted to provide an explanation, through the doctrine known as 'Original Sin', and many theologians have since questioned whether this is a proper interpretation of the Old Testament concept. What the story of Adam suggests is not that a single man once committed an offence, and then all of his descendants inherited that tendency: rather, it implies that humanity is 'sinning' all the time, and will continue to do so until God's creative act is completed.

It also suggests that the act of sinning becomes a part of the nature of the sinner. To use an analogy, our mothers used to tell us when we were children that if we persisted in 'making faces' we would 'stick like that'. What we did would turn into what we were. This is what is meant in that well known but much misunderstood passage:

> *'Be sure your sin will find you out'* (Numbers 32:23)

It does not mean 'Be sure your sin will be found out'. It means that your sin will expose what sort of person you are. You will be shown up for what you have become.

Sin does not rightly belong in true human nature

Yet it would be wrong to take this too far, and to imagine that human sinfulness is a proper part of human nature itself. In the Bible, sin is portrayed as alien to true human nature: it does not rightly belong there. It is an intrusion into what people really are. The narrative about Adam makes it plain that he does not sin because it is in his nature to do so. He is 'led astray by sin'.

His fault lies in his weakness – his tendency to prefer to do wrong rather than to do what is right. It lies also in his pride – that is to say, in his tendency to think of himself as completely autonomous and self-sufficient. When God places Adam in the Garden of Eden, Adam is told that everything is now his, except the tree which bears the forbidden fruit of the knowledge of good and evil. It is as if God were saying to him

> *'The whole world is yours, but its centre is not yours. That centre belongs to God alone, and to usurp it is to place yourself arrogantly on God's throne.'*

The whole of humanity is in this position, and thus there is another kind of unity evident. Just as mankind is one in the sense that all belong together, so also it is one in its weakness. We are bound up with each other in Creation, and we are also bound up with one another in the universality of 'sin'.

In the New Testament, St Paul takes up this idea of our corporate nature, and he does it in two ways. He does it by showing that

> *'all have sinned and fallen short of the glory of God (see Romans 3:23 and also Romans 5:12),*

and he also does it by showing that by entering into faith-union with Christ within the Church, people are re-united with one another in such a way that they become truly 'one':

> *'If one member suffers, all suffer together ... if one member is honoured, all rejoice together ...' (see 1 Corinthians 12:26)*

His point is that by virtue of Christ's creative and saving work, humanity is given back its true unity, as opposed to the false unity found in the common propensity to sinfulness.

But the corporate nature of human beings is such that it also allows room for individuality. Certainly we are bound up with each other, but at the same time we are ourselves, with our personal identities and personal characteristics. From time to time we find passages in the Bible where this individuality is stressed. For example, the prophet Ezekiel saw clearly that if too much emphasis was placed on the idea of corporate humanity and corporate sinfulness, then there could be no such thing as personal responsibility. Those who offended could all too easily blame others, and claim that it was not their own fault. The notion that corporate humanity cancelled out individual sinfulness or saintliness needed to be countered. If there was to be any genuine contrition by 'sinners', then there had to be room for an acknowledgement of one's own personal culpability:

> *'What do you mean by repeating this proverb concerning the land of Israel, "The parents have eaten sour grapes, and the children's teeth are set on edge"? As I live, says the Lord GOD, this proverb shall no more be used by you in Israel. Know that all lives are mine; the life of the parent as well as the life of the child is mine: it is only the person that sins that shall die ...'. (Ezekiel 18:2ff)*
>
> *'Yet you say, "Why should not the son suffer for the iniquity of the father?" When the son has done what is lawful and right, and has been careful to observe all my statutes, he shall surely live. The person who sins shall die. A child shall not suffer for the inquity of a parent, nor a parent suffer for the iniquity of a child; the righteousness of the righteous shall be his own, and the wickedness of the wicked shall be his own.' (Ezekiel 18:19–20)*

Love as the only lasting form of unity

According to St Paul, although humanity is united in a common bond of sin, this bond cannot last. What holds a Christian community together – and indeed the only thing that can bind everyone together – is LOVE. It is in that love that individuality and community become one and the same thing. The 'many' become the 'one'. Paul saw love as the key to true unity and as the only genuinely lasting virtue *(see 1 Corinthians 13:8)*. Love alone is capable of bearing and enduring everything – everything, that is, which would otherwise result in fragmentation and disunity. Not only does Paul appeal to Christians to love one another, and to continue to live in that unifying love-relationship: he also makes it plain that it is not ordinary human love which he is talking about, but the love of God himself as revealed and expressed in the person of Christ:

> *'God's love has been poured into our hearts through the Holy Spirit that has been given to us ...' (see Romans 5:1–5).*

Those who manifest the love of God in Christ find that they can bring their different gifts (that is, the things that mark them out as individuals) and use them in the common good, to build up the corporate life. They can share their differences, and find unity in their diversity:

> *'For just as the body is one and has many members, and all the members of the body, though many, are one body, so it is with Christ. For in the one Spirit we were all baptized into one body ...' (1 Corinthians 12:12ff)*

Paul's aim in preaching the Gospel was to proclaim this God-given unity, and to see it taking the place of the 'unity-in-sin' which characterised the human condition when God was left out.

POINTS FOR DISCUSSION

1. The mythological language of the Creation narrative (Genesis 2:4b ff) describes humanity as 'sinful'. Is there a more appropriate way of expressing this in modern terminology?
2. In what sense (or senses) can it be said that the whole human race is 'one'? What is it that binds us all together, apart from our biological similarities?
3. If we have all been 'born free', are there any limits to that freedom? Does freedom necessarily imply responsibility?
4. How can we balance our individuality against our corporateness? Can we be both independent and interdependent?

5. Do you agree with St Paul's assessment that everyone has sinned and fallen short of perfection? Or is this too much of a generalisation?
6. Is it really true that human beings are fully human only when they are within a community?
7. Is 'sin' the same thing as 'pride'?
8. What do you understand by Christian love, as distinct from any other kind of love? What are its special characteristics?

2 | Pain and Suffering

In the previous Study we noted how, in the Biblical literature, humanity is regarded as being corporate – that is to say, everyone is bound up with everyone else, and human beings are perceived as being part of one another. What happens to one, happens to all. This is a crucially important concept, because it provides the foundation for our understanding of the work of Christ, and for our appreciation of what is meant when he is referred to as the 'new Adam' (see Advent Study 2). In this second Lenten Study we now turn to examine what must be the most difficult of all problems for Christian faith, and that is the undeniable fact of the existence of suffering within universal human experience.

Suffering manifests itself in many forms, and it compels Christians to think very hard about aspects of their theology. For example, it challenges an over-simplistic Christian belief in a good God, since it is hard to accept that a benevolent and merciful Deity would ever permit suffering of any sort to take place. It also challenges Christian belief in God's power, because it seems reasonable to suppose that if God's 'almightiness' means that he is able to to everything, then he ought to be able to banish suffering altogether from his creation. It appears, at least on the surface, that we are faced with a choice between God's goodness and God's almightiness: if he is good, then the continued existence of suffering must be due to his inability to do anything about it. Alternatively, if he could eradicate it through the exercise of his divine power, but chooses not to do so, then we have to question his goodness, or look for some other answer to the problem.

Again, the experience of suffering seems to challenge Christian belief in God's justice, because to human eyes it often appears as if the people who suffer most are the very people who deserve it least. It looks as if suffering and misery are not distributed fairly. Then there are further difficulties concerning the distinctions between forms of suffering: for example, there is the kind which is brought upon oneself as a consequence of wrong-doing (as when a thief is caught and is sent to prison), but there is also the sort which follows upon natural causes (such as earthquakes or outbreaks of disease, where no-one can be directly blamed). These are often referred to as 'deserved suffering' and 'innocent suffering'. In the same vein, there are distinctions between levels or degrees of suffering, which often seem hard to understand. Mild forms of suffering do not appear to raise the same problems for faith as those which are extremely severe.

We will look at some of these issues here, but we cannot possibly do more than scratch the surface. What we can do, however, is to recognise that suffering is not just one single problem for religious faith: it raises very many distinct questions, and if we were to examine some of the other major religions of the world we would quickly see that those problems are often directly related to their various concepts of God's nature and purposes. The problems are not always seen in the same ways, and no single religion can be said to have 'solved' all of them. For the atheist, of course, the questions raised by the fact of suffering are very different, because there is no need to struggle with theological difficulties.

Is suffering a punishment?

In both the Old and the New Testaments there is ample evidence that people sometimes regarded human suffering as a punishment for sin. This is clearly the interpretation contained in the second narrative of creation *(Genesis 2:4b ff)*, where Adam and Eve are sentenced by God to lives of pain and discomfort, because they disobeyed his law. Adam will find that his work is arduous, and Eve will find that child-bearing is painful *(Genesis 3:14–19)*. In the New Testament, we find it openly said that physical disability (in this case, blindness) is popularly thought to be the consequence of sin:

> '*His disciples asked him "Rabbi, who sinned, this man or his parents, that he was born blind"?*' *(John 9:2)*

The Old Testament prophets constantly proclaimed their belief that national and individual sin would bring down the wrath of God, often in the form of pestilence or even invasion and oppression by some foreign power, which God would use as the instrument of his divine indignation. For example, the prophet Isaiah believed that the impending invasion by the Assyrian forces was God's way of expressing his anger at the wickedness of his people:

> '*Ah, Assyria, the rod of my anger – the club in their hands is my fury! Against a godless nation I send him, and against the people of my wrath I command him ...*' *(Isaiah 10:5ff)*

and in just the same way the later Babylonian Exile was understood to have been a punishment sent by God upon his disobedient people:

> '*Speak tenderly to Jerusalem and cry to her that she has served her term, that her penalty is paid, that she has received from the LORD's hand double for all her sins ...*' *(Isaiah 40:2)*

Behind this kind of thinking lay the principle of God's absolute righteousness. He would not and could not tolerate wickedness. Sin had to be seen to be followed by some kind of penalty. To ignore it would have been to condone it.

In a way, this interpretation of the cause of suffering offered a simple solution: offend against God, and you will be punished: do good, and you will not suffer. Nothing bad will ever happen to you. There is no shortage of Biblical examples of this strand of thought. For example, in the book of Psalms we find this:

> '*A thousand may fall at your side, ten thousand at your right hand, but it will not come near you. You will only look with*

your eyes and see the punishment of the wicked. Because you have made the LORD your refuge, the Most High your dwelling place, no evil shall befall you, no scourge come near your tent.' (Psalm 91:7 ff)

Innocent suffering

In the book of Job, however, we find something of a departure from this idea. Here, Job is presented as a saintly figure who has never disobeyed God – or, at least, he has no awareness of having offended. Even God himself is said to have regarded Job as innocent of any evildoing:

'Have you considered my servant Job? There is no one like him on the earth, a blameless and upright man who fears God and turns away from evil ...' (Job 2:3)

The theme of this book (which some scholars regard as being outside the mainstream of conventional Jewish religious thought) is that of the problem of innocent suffering. It attempts to discuss the difficult question of why it is that good people sometimes suffer, and it raises the problem of trying to understand the nature of God's justice. One answer which this book offers is that suffering constitutes a kind of divine test of faith, and the point is clearly brought out in the introductory prose section. Satan is portrayed as a cynical figure, who doubts whether Job would be able to sustain his saintliness if things went wrong for him:

'Does Job fear God for nothing? Have you not put a fence around him and his house and all that he has, on every side? You have blessed the work of his hands, and his possessions have increased in the land. But stretch out your hand now, and touch all that he has, and he will curse you to his face ...' (Job 1:9–11)

But the idea that suffering is a test of faith is not the only solution which this book offers. At another level, we find that Job's misery comes to an end only when he stops questioning God's justice. God seems to be saying to him 'I am God, and I can do whatever I wish. I have my own divine reasons, and they are nothing to do with you. The mystery of suffering is something you will never understand' *(see Job 42:1 ff)*. Here, the point is not that suffering can be understood as God's way of testing his people: it is that it cannot ever be understood at all, and must simply be accepted as a fact within God's created order.

'It will all be put right in the end'

Other Old Testament writers had also seen that the equation 'suffering = punishment for sin' was too simplistic. The simple observation of what was happening in real life was enough in itself to call that explanation into question, because good people were suffering, while bad people were apparently getting away with murder. The prophet Habakkuk was convinced that God would indeed bring down his wrath upon evil-doers, but he was at the same time puzzled by God's seeming inaction when wickedness prevailed over goodness:

> *'Your eyes are too pure to behold evil, and you cannot look on wrongdoing; why do you look on the treacherous, and are silent when the wicked swallow those more righteous than they?' (Habakkuk 1:13)*

But he went no further than asking the question, and in the end he contented himself with the thought that, sooner or later, the inequalities would be put right. God's justice would ultimately prevail, no matter how long it might take. In the meantime, he would continue to retain his faith. The final chapter of the book of Habakkuk is in the form of a psalm, and differs in some respects from the earlier section, but it aptly sums up the prophet's attitude towards the presence of suffering in the world:

> *'Though the fig tree does not blossom, and no fruit is on the vines; though the produce of the olive fails and the fields yield no food; though the flock is cut off from the fold and there is no herd in the stalls, yet I will rejoice in the LORD; I will exult in the God of my salvation.' (Habakkuk 3:17)*

In this kind of statement we see another approach to understanding the apparent injustice of suffering, which has been called the **eschatological** solution. This simply means that the inequalities in the distribution of suffering, though very evident in this present age, will be removed in God's good time, when all his purposes will be revealed in the 'last days'.

Vicarious suffering

We strike a very different note when we look at one of the ideas of the anonymous prophet who is generally known as Second Isaiah (or Deutero-Isaiah). He introduces a mysterious figure into his prophetic message, who will voluntarily accept the deserved sufferings of others, and endure their punishments for them. He will become a sacrificial figure – an 'offering for sin' *(see Isaiah 53:10)*, and just as he takes the wickedness of others upon himself, so also his goodness will be given to them:

> *'... upon him was the punishment that made us whole, and by his bruises we are healed ...'*
>
> *'The righteous one, my servant, shall make many righteous, and he shall bear their iniquities.' (Isaiah 53:5 and 53:11)*

In later Christian theology this 'servant' came to be identified with Jesus Christ, though contemporary Judaism insists that the reference is not to a single personality but to the Jewish community itself, acting in its role as God's mediator to the Gentile world. We can see how Christians, in the light of the experience of Christ's death, would want to find a solution to the problem of why he died, and the author of the letter to the Hebrews takes up this theme of a righteous man offering himself as a sacrifice for the sins of others:

> *'It is by God's will that we have been sanctified through the offering of the body of Jesus Christ once for all'.*
> *(Hebrews 10:10)*

He pictures Jesus as the perfect High Priest, offering himself as the perfect sacrifice which will satisfy God's divine justice and also make any further sacrifices unnecessary. In the Fourth Gospel, however, the author plays down the ritual aspect of sacrifice, and instead he represents the death of Jesus as an act of divine love:

> *'No-one has greater love than this, to lay down one's life for one's friends.' (John 15:13)*

> *'For God so loved the world that he gave his only Son, so that everyone who believes in him may not perish but may have eternal life' (John 4:16)*

All this raises a great many further questions which we cannot hope to answer here, but we shall explore some of them in the remaining Studies. In particular we shall look at the issues of Justice, Mercy and Forgiveness, and then, in the light of what we discover, we shall come back again to the Christian understanding of Sacrifice.

POINTS FOR DISCUSSION

1. Is suffering always to be regarded as negative? Does it have any positive value? For instance, was the writer George Eliot right to suggest that 'deep, unspeakable suffering may well be called a baptism, a regeneration, the initiation into a new state'? Does it really make people more noble? Or does it dehumanise them?

2. To what extent does the suffering of punishment serve to absolve the offender? Is punishment the same thing as vengeance?

3. Is it fair to say that the presence of suffering in the world forces us to choose between God's goodness and God's almightiness?

4. Was the writer of the book of Job getting close to the truth when he said that God alone has the answer to suffering?

5. If suffering is one of God's ways of righting wrong, why are Christians expected to alleviate it whenever they see it? Should some people be left to 'stew in their own juice'?

6. Does it make any sense to claim that someone can suffer on behalf of someone else? Can any examples of this be found in everyday life?
7. If suffering really is a test of faith, what kind of a God would want to check up on his people in this way?

3 | Justice, Mercy and Forgiveness

The three concepts of justice, mercy and forgiveness are central both to Biblical theology as a whole and also to the Christian understanding of the work of Jesus Christ. We shall examine them together in this Study, because in fact they are inseparable from one another.

Justice

One of the most dominant characteristics of God, as described in both the Old and the New Testaments, is his concern for justice – sometimes translated as 'righteousness'. He measures what is right and what is wrong, and in this sense he behaves like a judge. He also is said to dispense justice, in that he metes out punishments for wrongdoing. He expects his people to do what is right, and provides 'Torah' (guidance) so that they can know the difference between right and wrong. But righteousness is not merely something that God is said to demand from his people: it is also something which is part of his own divine nature. He is, by definition, a God of righteous judgment. He is not administering laws which have been determined elsewhere. They are *his* laws, and they have their origin in his very being. This is an altogether different concept from that of the ancient Greek world, where righteousness had its roots in mankind's own innate goodness – that is to say, in what is sometimes called our 'higher nature'. For the Hebrew mind, God's righteousness or justice consists in what God actually is, rather than in what he wants, though of course he will always be true to his nature, and will want what is right. Everything in the created order exhibits this truth:

> '*The heavens declare his righteousness, for God himself is judge.*' *(Psalm 50:6)*

and even he is bound by its requirements:

> 'Shall not the Judge of all the earth do what is just?'
> (Genesis 18:25)

When he calls his people to serve and to worship him, he expects that they will reflect that divine justice in their own lives, by doing what he has ordained to be right. Justice is never an abstract concept: it is something which is actually done in practice. The great King David in the Old Testament is said to have 'administered justice' throughout Israel *(see 2 Samuel 8:15)*, and this marked him out as someone who served God properly. The prophet Micah says that God has shown mankind the essence of goodness, and one of its main features is justice *(see Micah 6:8)*. Conversely, disobedience against God is perceived as injustice or unrighteousness, which always brings down God's divine wrath upon the offender. Those who would serve God properly are required to reflect his justice in their lives, and those who fail to do this are condemned, because God's nature prevents him from condoning injustice.

Sometimes, in both the Old and the New Testaments, justice is translated into social terms, and becomes something like 'equity' or 'fairness'. It was the manifest lack of this which prompted the prophet Amos to criticise his people for allowing inequalities to prevail. The poor always seemed to come off worst *(see Amos 5:11)*. Yet the people still believed themselves to be complying with God's requirements by going through the motions of sacrificial worship. Amos quickly put them right on this score:

> *'I hate, I despise your festivals, and I take no delight in your solemn assemblies ... but let justice roll down like waters, and righteousness like an everflowing stream.' (Amos 5:21ff)*

In the New Testament, the letter of James make much the same kind of point. Those who make social distinctions, at the expense of the poor, are considered to be false or evil judges *(see James 2:1–4)*.

God takes injustice or unrighteousness very seriously. It 'angers' him, because it stands in direct opposition to him, and contradicts his nature. He has to do something about it, because he cannot ignore it. At one level, the obvious response to injustice is to punish it, and there is no shortage of Biblical passages which illustrate this:

> '*I will punish the world for its evil, and the wicked for their iniquity; I will put an end to the pride of the arrogant, and lay low the insolence of tyrants ...*' (Isaiah 13:11)

> '*I will punish them for their ways, and repay them for their deeds ...*' (Hosea 4:9)

But, at a different level, alongside this very important Biblical insight there is another, which grows out of the equally important recognition that God is also a merciful and loving deity, who prefers to restore his people rather than to destroy them. This takes us directly into the concept of mercy as something which goes beyond raw justice.

Mercy

Biblically speaking, mercy is not a contradiction of justice, but of vengeance. If justice is understood as being close in meaning to righteousness, then the concept of mercy takes it a little further. Vengeance, when sought by ordinary people, is wrong: it is wrong because only God is thought to have the right to exact it *(see Romans 12:19)*, and it is also wrong because it lacks the crucial elements of mercy and love. It is selfish, and it ignores the needs of the offender in that it does not seek to redeem or reform him, but only to exact retribution from him. Vengeance is prompted by hatred, whereas mercy is prompted by love. Like justice, mercy is also one of God's personal characteristics: he is by his very nature 'gracious and merciful' *(see for example 2 Chronicles 30:9)*, and it is characteristic of him that he shows compassion:

> '*I will be gracious to whom I will be gracious, and will show mercy on whom I will show mercy ...*' (Exodus 33:19)

> '*But you, O Lord, are a God merciful and gracious, slow to anger and abounding in steadfast love and faithfulness.*'
> *(Psalm 86:15)*

Again, it is this very quality which God expects to see in those who emulate him:

> '*Blessed are the merciful*' *(Matthew 5:7)*
>
> '*Be merciful, just as your Father is merciful*' *(Luke 6:36)*

In the Gospel of Matthew, Jesus is reported as saying that the scribes and Pharisees have been hypocritical by professing an outward religion but neglecting the essential elements of justice and mercy *(see Luke 23:23)*. To show mercy, first of all one must apply judgment, and then follow it by the application of love (or, as some translations put it, lovingkindness). Thus the cause of justice is served by recognising and condemning what is wrong, and then the principle of mercy is further recognised, by acting out of love rather than out of a desire to seek retribution. Mercy is something which goes beyond justice, and is even capable of over-ruling it:

> '*For judgment will be without mercy to anyone who has shown no mercy; mercy triumphs over judgment.*' *(James 2:13)*

Forgiveness

Forgiveness is something that goes even beyond mercy. Mercy is the application of love towards the offender by not 'giving him what is coming to him', and by seeking his renewal rather than his destruction: but forgiveness includes a further ingredient – a willingness on the part of the innocent party to accept the cost of the offence. For example, if someone steals five pounds from me, and I genuinely forgive him, it costs me five pounds, because I have lost my money. If I demand to have it back from him, I may have expressed a willingness to overlook his offence, and to try to understand why he did it, but I have not genuinely forgiven him, because I am still wanting repayment, and therefore the matter is not fully settled.

Nor is forgiveness to be confused with tolerance. Tolerance means putting up with something, whereas forgiveness means paying for it. It is therefore the one who actually does the forgiving – the 'injured party' – who suffers most of all. The seventeenth century English poet John Dryden summed it up neatly:

> *'Forgiveness to the injured does belong;*
> *But they ne'er pardon, who have done the wrong.'*
> (Dryden, **The Conquest of Canada**, written 1670)

Forgiveness also carries with it a readiness to preserve or continue a relationship which otherwise would have been broken by the original offence. My friend who steals my money is at the same time destroying our friendship, and although I might tolerate the loss of my money, I do not genuinely forgive him unless I am prepared to re-establish the broken relationship itself. But now there is a difference in that renewed relationship: by stealing from me, he has shown that he does not care much for my feelings. He was prepared to hurt me by his theft, and to lose our friendship for the sake of what he took from me. So now, if our relationship is to be restored, I must recognise that it is one-sided. I must love him more than he loves me. That is what forgiveness will necessarily entail. It means putting the whole incident away – not 'forgetting' it, because it is too important for that, but no longer allowing it to make any difference.

There is, therefore, a very close connection between forgiveness and reconciliation, which is brought out clearly in the writings of St Paul in the New Testament. His view is that the whole of the human race has offended against God, and thus has broken the close bond which was established by God at creation. So, in Paul's understanding, the work of Christ consisted of a healing process, or a reconciliation in which God did the forgiving. The actual Greek word which is translated as 'reconciliation' appears only in Paul's letters, and even there it is found in only two significant places:

> *'For if while we were enemies, we were reconciled to God through the death of his Son, much more surely, having been reconciled, will we be saved by his life.' (Romans 5:10)*

> *'All this is from God, who reconciled us to himself through Christ, and has given us the ministry of reconciliation; that is, in Christ God was reconciling the world to himself, not counting their trespasses against them, and entrusting the message of reconciliation to us.' (2 Corinthians 5:18ff)*

We can also find something of the same idea in the letter to the Ephesians:

> *'But now in Christ Jesus you who once were far off have been brought near by the blood of Christ. For he is our peace; in his flesh he has made both groups into one and has broken down the dividing wall, the hostility between us.' (Ephesians 2:13–14)*

This reference to the 'blood of Christ' is, of course, the language of the sacrificial system, and so it is to the idea of sacrifice that we must turn in our next Study.

POINTS FOR DISCUSSION

1. If justice has its origins in the nature of God himself, and not in mankind's own sense of right and wrong, are we to conclude that those who do not believe in God have no proper awareness of true morality?

2. Is justice the same thing as 'fair play'?

3. Is there a danger that 'mercy' might destroy 'justice'? Must we always be compassionate, or are there times when compassion gets in the way of justice? What is a Christian to make of the saying that 'Justice must not only be done: it must also be seen to be done'?

4. If we forgive someone, are we really telling them that their offence did not matter? Can we be said to have genuinely forgiven them if we keep on reminding them of their offence?

5. Do you agree that true forgiveness is costly to the one who does the forgiving? What do you think Jesus meant when he taught his disciples to pray 'Forgive us our trespasses, as we forgive those who trespass against us'? Was he implying that God's own forgiveness is conditional?

6. Is there such a thing as an unforgiveable sin?

4 Sacrifice

The word 'sacrifice' has a strange old-fashioned look about it. It seems to relate to primitive religious customs such as the slaughtering of certain animals for ritual purposes, and to out-moded and crude ideas of a God who likes to be pampered by receiving gifts from his worshippers. In the Free Churches (i.e. Methodists, Baptists, United Reformed, etc.), this sacrificial aspect of Christian worship has to some extent been toned down by the removal of the altar from church buildings, and its replacement by a simple Communion Table. The concept of a priest who officiates at a sacrifice has also gone from these denominations, and in its place has come the idea of a 'minister'. In the Anglican and Roman Catholic traditions, however, the altar is still central, and the Sacrament of Holy Communion (the Eucharist or the Mass) is still interpreted mainly as a sacrificial act, at which a priest officiates.

As far as the Christian festival of Easter is concerned, the terminology of sacrifice is used a great deal in relation to the work of Christ, and it appears in many well-known Easter hymns:

> 'Ride on! ride on in majesty!
> The winged squadrons of the sky
> Look down with sad and wondering eyes
> To see the approaching sacrifice.'
>
> *(Henry Hart Milman, 1791–1868)*

> 'He died that we might be forgiven,
> He died to make us good,
> That we might go at last to heaven,
> Saved by His precious blood.'
>
> *(Cecil Frances Alexander, 1818–1895)*

In modern times the concept of sacrifice has often been modified to one of self-discipline, and it has frequently been suggested that a sacrifice takes place whenever someone 'gives something up'. The season of Lent itself is commonly treated in this way, that is, as an opportunity for Christians to share sympathetically in Christ's sacrificial sufferings by deliberately avoiding certain enjoyable practices, or by abstaining from acts of self-indulgence. But this falls far short of what 'sacrifice' really means, and in this Study we shall examine the concept more closely.

The sacrificial system

Many religions have sacrificial systems, and Christianity is no exception. The basis of the Christian understanding of sacrifice is to be found in the Old Testament, where it is seen to have several meanings. At one level it was simply a ritualised way of offering gifts to God, in the same way as someone might give presents as symbols of love and affection, or as an expression of gratitude. Such gifts were known as 'freewill offerings' or 'offerings of praise', usually prompted by an awareness that the worshipper had himself first received a gift from God and therefore also representing an element of thanksgiving:

> *'Then you shall keep the festival of weeks for the LORD your God, contributing a freewill offering in proportion to the blessing that you have received from the LORD your God.' (Deuteronomy 16:10)*

Some sacrificial offerings were made because the worshipper had taken a religious vow, and the sacrifice was a physical sign that the promise was being kept. These are generally referred to as 'votive offerings'.

Giving God what is already his

At another level, a sacrificial offering would be intended to acknowledge the sovereignty of God over the whole of creation, and to give him what in principle already belongs to him. Thus the firstborn of the herds, or the first crop of the fields, or even the first male child in the family would be symbolically laid before God. If it was the offering of a child, then that child would afterwards be 'redeemed', that is to say, purchased back into the family by another kind of ritualised payment, but he would still be regarded as having been dedicated into God's service:

> *'... you shall set apart to the LORD all that first opens the womb ... Every firstborn male among your children you shall redeem.' (Exodus 13:11ff)*

We can see this principle in operation in the story of the child Samuel in the Old Testament. Hannah give birth to a child after having been barren for a long time. As a thank-offering, and also because Samuel is her firstborn son, she takes him to the Temple and offers him to God. He is 'lent to the LORD' *(see 1 Samuel 1:1ff)*.

This was an acknowledgement of God's ownership of the life that he had created, though the custom was also linked with the story of the Exodus from Egypt, when God is said to have miraculously preserved all the firstborn Hebrew boys during his confrontation with Pharaoh *(see Exodus 12:12ff)*, and thereby 'claimed' their lives.

Putting things right

Another kind of sacrificial offering was that which was plainly intended to placate God, and to turn away his anger. Such offerings did not always serve precisely the same purpose: some were sacrifices for sin, and were meant as a kind of expiation to take the guilt away *(see, for example, Leviticus 17:11)*, and others were intended to make reparation for an offence *(see Leviticus 5:14–16)*. The distinctions between these were not always very clear, but it is evident that they were all based upon the fundamental belief that when a wrong was committed, either against God or against one's neighbour, something had to be done to put things right. The matter could not merely be left alone.

What shall I give him?

As the sacrificial system developed over the centuries, more and more complexities were introduced. There was a wide range of offerings made, depending upon the nature and purpose of the actual sacrifice. Animals and vegetables were involved, and the correct mode of their preparation was carefully set out in the priestly books of instruction. What was common to virtually all of them, however, was that the gift must be pure and clean – worthy of being given to God, who would not accept sacrifices that were imperfect or inadequate. To give God the 'left-overs', or the things that were cheaply-acquired or no longer needed, was regarded as highly offensive, because a sacrifice was never merely a token gesture. It was costly, or else it had no meaning.

Sacrifice a a communion meal

One important aspect of the sacrificial system was the way in which it often represented a kind of 'communion with God'. In the eastern world it was generally accepted that when someone eats a meal with someone else – that is to say, 'shares bread' (which is what the word 'companion' originally meant), then an important bond is created between them. To eat from the same loaf or from the same table symbolised a serious relationship. Casual acquaintances or strangers never did this: they might be given food, but to share in the family meal at the family table was a very different matter. Thus, if a sacrifice was made at which the offering was given to God but also eaten by the worshipper (or by the priest on the worshipper's behalf), then it was believed that a new and deeply intimate relationship had been established with God. God and his people were sharing the same food. Here, of course, we can see immediate links with the Christian sacrament of Holy Communion.

The seriousness of sacrifice

What mattered most of all, in every kind of sacrifice, was that the worshipper should make his offering seriously. His offering should in some way be a symbol of himself. God did not want substitutes for the real thing: he wanted the sacrifice of the worshipper, and not a 'cheap imitation'. The very complexity of the sacrificial system, and the importance attached to the person of the priest, shows how seriously a religious sacrifice was meant to be taken. We can find in the Old Testament numerous passages stressing the fact that God did not want sacrifices for their own sake, but only if they genuinely embodied the offering of the worshipper:

> *'Has the LORD as great delight in burnt offerings and sacrifices as in obeying the voice of the LORD? Surely, to obey is better than sacrifice, and to heed than the fat of rams ...'*
> *(1 Samuel 15:22)*

> *'For I desire steadfast love and not sacrifice, the knowledge of God rather than burnt offerings ...' (Hosea 6:6)*

Somehow the worshipper had to be 'in' the sacrifice, and to go through the motions of offering it, but without any sincerity, was worse than not offering it at all. We catch echoes of this principle in St Paul's admonition to the Corinthian Christians, when he chided them for the casual way in which they celebrated the Lord's Supper and told them that if it meant so little to them, and they could not 'discern the body' of Christ within it, then they might as well stay at home to eat *(see 1 Corinthians 11:17ff)*.

The letter to the Hebrews

It is in the letter to the Hebrews in the New Testament that we find the most explicit statements about Jesus Christ in the context of ritual sacrifice. The unknown writer, evidently steeped in Jewish custom, presents Christ as fulfilling all the necessary conditions for the perfect sacrifice. First, Jesus is portrayed as the ideal High Priest: he was properly appointed *(see Hebrews 5:5–6)*, and he possessed the right qualifications in that he was

> *'holy, blameless, undefiled, separated from sinners, and exalted above the heavens ...' (see Hebrews 7:26ff)*

The sacrifice which Christ offered was also superior to any other kind, because (unlike those offered by ordinary priests) it was complete, and did not need ever again to be repeated. Furthermore, because Christ is alive for ever, he holds his priestly office permanently *(see Hebrews 7:23–24)*. Most important of all, however, is the fact that Christ offered the ideal sacrifice: it was not bulls or goats that were offered to God, but Christ's very self. He fulfilled the demands of God which the Old Testament prophets had proclaimed, that the one who offers the sacrifice must also become the sacrifice *(see Hebrews 9:11ff and 10:8ff)*. Christ did not offer substitutes: he offered himself.

This kind of ritual and cultic language seems altogether alien to contemporary ears, but when it is set in its proper context it illustrates very clearly the Christian belief that the work of Christ was essentially that of enabling people to 'get right with God'.

POINTS FOR DISCUSSION

1. Does the language of the ancient sacrificial system of Israel mean anything in the modern world? If not, how could its central meaning be conveyed in contemporary terminology?

2. If God requires some sort of 'payment' in order to restore the broken relationship between himself and humanity, what are we to make of the teaching that we have been reconciled by his 'free grace'?

3. What do you think St Paul meant when he appealed to the Christians in Rome to present their bodies as a living sacrifice, holy and acceptable to God *(Romans 12:1)*?

4. Is there any truth in the suggestion that a sacrifice is really no more than a bribe paid to God, to buy him off?

5. If Christ's sacrifice was made once and for all, why is it that the Church goes on repeating it in the celebration of the Eucharist (Holy Communion)?

6. **Why have the Free Churches removed the altar from their church buildings, and dispensed with the office of a priest?**

5   Obedience

From time to time in our previous Studies we have made reference to the theme of humanity's disobedience of God's laws, and the consequences of that disobedience. We have also noted the way in which Jesus is frequently depicted in the New Testament as having been 'obedient', even to the point of giving up his life. In this Study we turn to explore the notion of 'obedience' itself, especially in relation to the suffering of Christ, but before we do so we need to note that obedience, in the Biblical tradition, has nothing to do with servility or submissiveness – characteristics which were never regarded as admirable because they suggest a lack of personal courage. Unfortunately, the virtue of obedience has become confused in many people's minds with the idea of weakness or humility, and consequently it has lost a good deal of its force. The image of Jesus as a baby who never cried, and as a quiet, passive kind of man, who was so 'nice' that he never upset anyone, and even allowed himself to be led unprotesting to the cross, dies very hard indeed. Certainly there are some passages in the New Testament where that sort of picture seems to be presented, as, for example:

> 'Take my yoke upon you, and learn from me; for I am gentle and humble in heart, and you will find rest for your souls.' (Matthew 11:29)

but these have to be balanced against other passages which show Jesus in a very different light:

> 'But turning and looking at his disciples, he rebuked Peter and said, "Get behind me, Satan!" ...' (Mark 8:33)

> 'Making a whip of cords, he drove all of them out of the temple, both the sheep and the cattle. He also poured out the coins of the money changers and overturned their tables ...' (John 2:15)

It is extremely difficult to make judgments about Jesus's personal temperament, because the Gospel accounts of his life have been so powerfully affected by the writers' theological intentions. Each of them, in his own way, wanted to present Jesus as being fully human and yet also as someone who embodied the very nature of God. This inevitably conditioned what they said about him. But the fact that he attracted so much public attention, and was able to draw such large crowds to hear him preach, makes it impossible to regard him as a docile and self-effacing figure who never stepped out of line. Indeed, his powerful criticisms of certain religious attitudes mark him out as a man with strong convictions and the necessary courage to stand by them. He was manifestly not the sort who was prepared to stand back and let things happen to him without protest.

But if 'obedience', in the Biblical sense, does not imply a passive acceptance of whatever comes, then what is it? We pick up an important clue, yet again, in the second creation narrative of the book of Genesis *(Genesis 2:4ff)*, where 'Adam' is instructed not to eat of the fruit of the tree of knowledge of good and evil. He disobeys that instruction, and is punished, along with Eve. The story illustrates the fundamental Hebrew principle that if humankind is to be as God intended, and is to fulfil God's purpose, then obedience to God's law is essential. It is obeying *God* which matters, and not simply submitting in an unthinking way to any kind of authority. When Paul, in the New Testament era, told the Christian congregation in Rome that they must submit to the political regime, he explained that this was because it had been placed in authority by God:

> *'Let every person be subject to the governing authorities;*
> *for there is no authority except from God, and those*
> *authorities that exist have been instituted by God.*
> *Therefore whoever resists authority resists what God*
> *has appointed, and those who resist will incur judgment.'*
> *(Romans 13:1–2)*

The obedient son

The idea of obedience as the hallmark of true sonship is very prominent in both the Old and the New Testaments, and it has its roots in the Biblical concept of the Fatherhood of God. Contrary to popular opinion, the Old Testament has very little to say about God as 'our Heavenly Father' in a personal or individual sense. That was something which Jesus himself took up and developed later on. What the Old Testament does expose, however, is the belief that God is the Father of the whole nation of Israel, having taken it upon himself to enter into a special kind of covenant-relationship with them. In the narrative of the great 'divine rescue' from slavery in Egypt, which has come to be known as the Exodus, God adopts the Hebrew people as his children, and thinks of them corporately as his son *(see Hosea 11:1)*. But in order to remain in that intimate relationship, they in their turn must display the primary characteristic of the ideal son – which is the virtue of obedience. That is precisely what 'sonship' entails – doing the will of the father, and not merely pleasing oneself. The good and true son is also the obedient and dutiful son.

We can see this teaching clearly illustrated in the book of Proverbs:

> *'Hear, my child, your father's instruction ...' (Proverbs 1:6, also 4:1, 6:20, etc.)*
>
> *'A wise child makes a glad father ...' (Proverbs 15:20)*
>
> *'Listen to your father who begot you ...' (Proverbs 23:22)*,

and these admonitions, though here set out in the very practical context of Wisdom literature, accurately reflect the religious principle of obedience to God. Those who disobey the divine Law have cut themselves off from the covenant-relationship, and are therefore no longer members of the family of God.

Perhaps the best illustration of this is to be found in the New Testament, in the famous parable of the Prodigal Son *(see Luke*

15:11ff). A man has two sons, one of whom breaks away from the family environment and wastes his inheritance, while the other stays loyally at home. When the wastrel comes to his senses and decides to return, he is welcomed by his father, and given back his true status as a son; but his elder brother, who had stayed at home, is offended by this, and remonstrates with his father, arguing that he has not been treated fairly. His case is a simple one:

> *'For all these years I have been working like a slave for you, and I have never disobeyed your command ...' (Luke 15:29)*

Evidently he is upset because his 'obedience' has not, after all, given him any advantage over his delinquent brother – whom he describes to his father as 'this son of yours' *(Luke 15:30)*, and he has to be reminded that 'this brother of yours' has come home *(Luke 15:32)*. The father then makes it plain that the son's obedience has not been overlooked, despite outward appearances:

> *'Son, you are always with me, and all that is mine is yours ...' (Luke 15:31),*

a phrase which is immediately reminiscent of a passage in the fourth Gospel, where these words are attributed to Jesus:

> *'All that the Father has is mine ...' (John 16:15)*

The parable of the Prodigal Son, as it stands in the Gospel of Luke, looks very much like a piece of polemic against those Jews who had accepted Jesus as the Messiah but who were not willing to allow that God's love extended as far as the Gentiles. The younger son is the symbol of the typical Gentile. He lives in a foreign country, he disregards the Law, and he even keeps pigs. The elder son is the model Jew. He stays at home, works hard, and (most important of all) he is obedient to his father. What he still cannot do, however, is to bring himself to recognise that the Gentile, when he too becomes 'obedient' to God, is his brother.

It is in the fourth Gospel that the idea of Jesus as the obedient son is most powerfully developed, though it is also strongly present in the letter to the Hebrews. Throughout his book, John is at pains to demonstrate the one-ness of Jesus with God, always doing God's will and never swerving from the course that has been set for him. It is John alone who records the words of Jesus:

> *'Jesus said to them, "My food is to do the will of him who sent me and to complete his work" ' (John 4:34)*

> *'I can do nothing on my own. As I hear, I judge; and my judgement is just, because I seek to do not my own will but the will of him who sent me.' (John 5:30)*

But we also find the three Synoptic Gospels preserving Jesus's statement:

> *'My father, if it is possible, let this cup pass from me; yet not what I want but what you want ...' (Matthew 26:39, see also Mark 14:36 and Luke 22:42)*

The suffering servant

Alongside this imagery of the obedient son we have to place that of the mysterious Suffering Servant, described so graphically in the book of Isaiah in the Old Testament *(see Isaiah 53)*. We have already looked at this passage in an earlier Study, but here we can note that it played a significant part in shaping Christian thought about the meaning of Christ's suffering and death. In particular it came to be used in the context of his willingness to do God's will, at whatever cost:

> *'He was oppressed, and he was afflicted, yet he did not open his mouth; like a lamb that is led to the slaughter, and like a sheep that before its shearers is silent, so he did not open his mouth ... Yet it was the will of the LORD to crush him with pain.' (Isaiah 53:7 and 10)*

What comes out of all this is the very clear teaching of the early

Church that when Jesus was put to death on the cross, apparently without complaint, he accepted it not because he was too docile and gentle to resist or to stand up for himself, but because he was fully aware that it was the will of God. His death was not only an act of sacrifice: it was also an act of obedience, which in itself provided (to the eye of faith) plain evidence that here indeed was God's true son.

POINTS FOR DISCUSSION

1. In the light of our understanding of Christ as 'obedient unto death', how are we to understand our own Christian obedience? Must a Christian accept whatever comes as being the will of God?
2. Before we can obey the will of God, we have to be certain of what it is that he wants from us. How *can* we know God's will?
3. Must Christian obedience always lead to suffering?
4. If it was the will of God that his own son should suffer, what does this imply about God himself? What sort of a father wants this for his son? Can we still look upon God as a 'loving' father?
5. What do you understand to be the difference between passivism and pacifism? Was Jesus a pacifist?

6 The Death of Christ

Jesus's trials and crucifixion

The actual circumstances of Jesus's trial and execution have never seriously been called into question. The evidence contained in the New Testament is strong – far stronger than that relating to the deaths of many other historical figures. He was arrested at night, in the Garden of Gethsemane *(Mark 14:32–50 and parallel passages)*, having been betrayed by Judas Iscariot, one of his own disciples. He then underwent two trials. The first was initiated by the Jewish leaders, headed by the High Priest Caiaphas *(Matthew 26:57ff)*, where he was pronounced guilty of blasphemy, an offence which they considered to be deserving of death *(Matthew 26:65–66)*. The Jews, however, being themselves subject to the power of the Roman law, did not have the authority to carry out an execution, so Jesus was then handed over to the Roman governor, Pontius Pilate *(Matthew 27:1–2)*. The charges made against Jesus at this second hearing were apparently numerous *(Matthew 27:13ff)*, but the only one which would warrant capital punishment was the political offence of seeking to usurp the position of Caesar. Pilate questioned Jesus, realised the true motives of the Jewish leaders, and came to the personal conclusion that he had done no wrong under Roman law. However, Pilate's brief was to ensure that peace was maintained in his territory, and he foresaw that if he allowed Jesus to go free he would almost certainly have a riot on his hands. So he agreed to the execution, having failed to appease the crowd by suggesting a pardon for Jesus under the amnesty granted at Passover festival time. Jesus was then taken away to Pilate's headquarters, and prepared for crucifixion, but first of all he was subjected to cruel mockery, which included dressing him up in imitation regal robes and pretending to offer him obeisance.

He was crucified along with two other law-breakers, one on either side of him, and a statement of his alleged offence was fastened above his head. The details of what was written on this notice are mentioned in the New Testament, but with some inconsistency. 'This is Jesus, the King of the Jews' *(Matthew 27:37)*, or 'The King of the Jews' *(Mark 15:26)*, or 'This is the King of the Jews' *(Luke 23:39)*, or 'Jesus of Nazareth, the King of the Jews' *(John 19:19)*. The inconsistencies are of little importance, since none of them is likely to be precisely accurate. In Roman custom it was normal to give much more detail than this, and the writers of the Gospels were probably less concerned with accuracy than with their desire to affirm the true nature of the man who was being executed.

The crucifixion itself involved nailing Jesus to a wooden stake – almost certainly cross-shaped rather than T-shaped – and leaving him there until he died. This would have been carried out by Roman soldiers, and not by Jews, though the Jews did have the right to remove his body afterwards and give him a proper burial according to their laws *(see Deuteronomy 21:22–23)*. It was one of Jesus's followers, Joseph of Arimathea, who asked Pontius Pilate for permission to take the body of Jesus away. He wrapped it in the usual grave-clothes, and placed it in a new tomb which had been cut out of solid rock. The tomb was then sealed *(see Mark 15:1–47 and Matthew 27:57–60)*.

'In accordance with the scriptures'

There is no good reason to doubt any of these particular details, but there is good reason to believe that the tradition out of which they came had, at a very early stage, been overlaid with theological commentary. Specifically, it seems more than likely that popular reflection upon Psalm 22, Psalm 69, and Isaiah 53 had coloured the way in which the crucifixion story was preserved and reported. It has often been noted that the actual account of the crucifixion, in all of the Gospels, is given in a remarkably matter-of-fact and impersonal way, but interspersed with the 'facts' we find clear references (in some places almost direct quotations) linking the narrative with the Old Testament passages mentioned above. For example:

> *'They gave me poison for food, and for my thirst they gave me vinegar to drink ...' (Psalm 69:21, compare with Mark 15:36)*
>
> *'Let their eyes be darkened so that they cannot see ...' (Psalm 69:23, compare with Mark 15:33)*
>
> *'My God, my God, why have you forsaken me?' (Psalm 22:1, compare with Mark 15:34)*
>
> *'They divide my garments among themselves, and for my clothing they cast lots ...' (Psalm 22:18, compare with Mark 15:24)*
>
> *'He was oppressed, and he was afflicted, yet he did not open his mouth; like a lamb that is led to the slaughter, and like a sheep that before its shearers is silent, so he did not open his mouth ...' (Isaiah 53:7, compare with Mark 15:1–5)*

It could, of course, be argued that these close similarities in points of detail were not 'read back' into the event, but actually describe what happened, thus proving that the Old Testament prophecies were being literally fulfilled: indeed, that is precisely how they were explained in the days before the coming of modern critical scholarship. But it is now much easier for us to recognise that here is one of many instances in the New Testament where the writers have embodied Old Testament ideas in the narrative in order to demonstrate their conviction that Christ's suffering and death were a part of God's eternal plan, and that everything was indeed happening in accordance with the Scriptures.

Was Jesus really dead?

The account of the burial of Jesus, which looks unimportant in itself and contains none of the Old Testament allusions which we find in the story of the crucifixion, was nevertheless very important for the first Christians. It was of crucial importance that they should be able to establish that Jesus was indeed dead, since if there was even the slightest chance that he was still alive when taken from the cross, then their belief in his resurrection would be undermined and their 'good news' would lose its force. They were not preaching a message of 'recovery', but of 'resurrection'. Their Lord had not managed to evade death: he had experienced it, and he had also conquered it. It is in the Gospel of Matthew that we catch a glimpse of the disputes over what had really happened, and the alternative explanations:

> *'Command the tomb to be made secure until the third day; otherwise his disciples may go and steal him away, and tell the people, 'He has been raised from the dead,' and the last deception would be worse than the first ...' (Matthew 27:64)*

Unlike the story of the raising of Jairus's daughter *(see Mark 5:21ff)*, there is never any hint that Jesus might not after all have been dead. In the case of the little girl, it is said that Jairus was notified of his daughter's death by a group of people who had come from the house where she was lying *(Mark 5:35)*, but Jesus himself contradicted this:

> *'Why do you make a commotion and weep? The child is not dead but sleeping ...' (Mark 5:39)*

However, the death of Jesus is said to have been attested by numerous witnesses, notably some women who had followed the whole series of events, and who had watched his interment closely *(see Mark 15:47 and Luke 23:55)*. There could be no doubt about his death.

How could the Messiah be dead?

But in affirming the death of Jesus there came a deeper problem, reflected in the closing part of the Gospel of Luke. The author describes how two followers of Jesus were walking together towards the village of Emmaus, after the crucifixion had taken place. They were discussing what had happened, and the essence of their problem was given in just a single sentence:

> *'But we had hoped that he was the one to redeem Israel.'*
> *(Luke 24:21)*

Their difficulty lay in understanding how it could be that the Messiah was dead. Did he not have God with him? Was he not the son of God? Did his death not disqualify him from Messiahship? This problem was to exercise the minds of many Christian thinkers later on, as the Church's theology was worked out in greater detail. If Jesus was truly God, did the crucifixion of the man Jesus also imply the death of God himself? Had God died on the cross? As we shall see in our next Study, the doctrine of the resurrection provided a solution, in that it proclaimed that Christ lived even after death: but it still left open the awkward question of how God himself could be said to have 'died' By emphasising their conviction that God *lived* in Christ, the early Christians inevitably brought upon themselves the necessity of showing how it was that he also *died* in Christ. The solution seemed to lie in saying that God had indeed suffered through the crucifixion of Jesus, just as any father suffers anguish at the death of his son. But human death is not the same thing as the destruction of the life of God itself, which is beyond death. The resurrection demonstrated not only that Christ had conquered death, but also that he was indeed – and always would be – 'alive to God'. It was the resurrection which proved, rather than disproved, the claims of Jesus's Messiahship. This is why, as we have previously seen, St Paul based his Gospel upon his experience of the post-resurrection Christ, and why he was able to say that it was:

> *'... the gospel concerning (God's) Son, who was descended from David according to the flesh and was declared to be the Son of God with power according to the spirit of holiness by resurrection from the dead, Jesus Christ our Lord ...'*
> *(Romans 1:3–4)*

POINTS FOR DISCUSSION

1. How much importance do Christians attach to the actual means of Jesus's death? Could there still be Christian faith if Jesus had lived longer and then died from natural causes? Did he *have* to be killed by crucifixion?

2. It is sometimes said that traditional Christianity has placed too much emphasis upon the crucifixion, at the expense of the resurrection of Christ, and has frequently been guilty of making an extremely cruel death into something noble and majestic. Do you agree?

3. Should we really blame Pontius Pilate for bringing about the death of Jesus by being too weak to defend him? Or should we blame Judas Iscariot for betraying Jesus? After all, was it not all part of God's will that Jesus should die? Were these men not instruments of God?

4. How can it be said that God 'suffered' in the crucifixion of Jesus? Is it not true that God is beyond suffering?

5. 'The crucifixion of Jesus, and the claims that he rose again from the dead, are irrelevant to Christian belief. The important thing is that his *teachings* shall live on, and that they shall be put into practice.' Is this true?

7 The Resurrection of Christ

In this penultimate Study we turn to the most important of all Christian teachings – the doctrine of the resurrection of Christ. This, in essence, is the claim that after he had been put to death, Jesus rose again from the grave.

The most natural question which comes immediately to mind is 'Did it really happen?', and that is where our Study has to begin. We can start by noting the nature and the force of the documentary evidence, which is entirely confined to the New Testament. All of the four Gospels record that the grave in which the body of Jesus had been laid after his crucifixion was later found to be empty, the stone sealing the entrance having been rolled away *(see Mark 16:1ff, Matthew 28:1ff, Luke 24:1ff, and John 20:1ff)*. This, of course, is not in itself evidence of a resurrection: a much more logical explanation would have been that the body of Jesus had simply been removed, and that is in fact what was affirmed at the time by the Jewish authorities:

> 'You must say, 'His disciples came by night and stole him away while we were asleep' ... and this story is still told among the Jews to this day' (Matthew 28:13–14)

The resurrection appearances

Matthew goes on to say, however, that after the discovery of the empty tomb, the risen Jesus met with the two women who had first visited the grave, and told them to instruct the disciples to go on to Galilee, where they also would see him. The account of that meeting between the resurrected Christ and his disciples forms the end of Matthew's Gospel. But some scholars have been reluctant to take this account as a piece of factual history. They prefer to see it as a piece of 'doctrinal commentary' added retrospectively, arguing in particular that it contains a direct reference to the doctrine of the Trinity, which could hardly have been something which Jesus would quote *(see Matthew 28:19)*.

But Matthew's Gospel is not the only one which describes post-resurrection appearances by Jesus. According to the Gospel of John, the risen Christ appeared mysteriously to his disciples in a locked room, where he spoke with them and showed them the injuries which he had sustained at the crucifixion. A similar experience is said to have taken place a week later, this time involving the disciple Thomas, whose disbelief was countered when Jesus invited him to reach out and touch the injuries. But again there have been some scholars who regard this as another doctrinal addition. They point out that, on each occasion, the appearance took place on what is described as 'the first day of the week' – a detail which has prompted them to link it with the later Christian custom of meeting regularly on 'the Lord's Day' in order to engage in worship and to seek communion with Christ *(see John 20:1ff)*.

There is also another account in the fourth Gospel of what purports to be an appearance of the risen Christ, and this is contained in the final chapter *(see Chapter 21:1ff)*. Here, Jesus is said to have 'shown himself' to his disciples by the sea of Tiberias, when they were fishing. They had caught nothing, until Jesus advised them to cast their nets on the other side of the boat – whereupon they could hardly cope with the number of fish that were in the net. Jesus is then recognised, and when they had come ashore they all shared a meal of bread and fish. There follows a strange account of Jesus issuing a second 'call of discipleship' to Peter.

We cannot, in this brief discussion, deal with all the issues raised here, but we can note that many scholars have judged this chapter to be out of place, and some are also convinced that it came from a different author. The previous chapter (Chapter 20) is clearly the true ending of the Gospel, and this one appears to have been added afterwards. It is therefore unsafe for us to regard this as a definite instance of a resurrection appearance by

Christ, though of course there are many who would wish to treat it as such.

In the Gospel of Luke, we find an account of a mysterious meeting between the risen Jesus and two of his followers, one of them identified as Cleopas *(see Luke 24:13ff)*. In this narrative, the two men are expressing their disappointment that their hopes had been dashed by the crucifixion. They had believed that Jesus was the Messiah, but now everything had gone wrong. To make things even worse, they had heard the rumour about how the grave had been found empty, and that Jesus was alive, but when some of their friends had gone to check on this they had again been disappointed because they had failed to see the resurrected Jesus. Luke then goes on to describe how these disillusioned disciples were reassured by Christ, who explained to them how it was that all these things had happened in accordance with God's purposes.

Yet, once again, some scholars have regarded this narrative as a kind of summary of early Christian teaching, rather than as a piece of factual reporting. They prefer to treat it as a highly-concentrated account of how primitive Christianity coped with the problem of reconciling the death of Jesus with the belief that he was indeed the true Messiah. They also point out that the latter part of this narrative – describing how Jesus went home with these two disciples and shared a meal with them *(see Luke 24:28ff)* – looks suspiciously like a modified picture of a very early Communion service *(see especially Luke 28:30)*, embodying the more developed Christian doctrine that the risen Christ now meets with his people through the medium of the sacrament. It is not impossible that the breakfast meal described in the closing chapter of John's Gospel, discussed above, also comes into this category.

Only two of the New Testament writers actually claimed that they had personally seen Jesus alive after his crucifixion. One was Paul in his correspondence with the Corinthian church:

> '*Am I not free? Am I not an apostle? Have I not seen Jesus our Lord? ...*' *(1 Corinthians 9:1)*
>
> '*Last of all, as to one untimely born, he appeared also to me ...*' *(1 Corinthians 15:8)*

and the other was the author of the book of Revelation, who described the experience as a 'vision':

> '*... and in the midst of the lampstands I saw one like the Son of Man, clothed with a long robe and with a golden sash across his chest ...*' *(Revelation 1:13)*

Neither of these is of much help: Paul could be referring to his so-called conversion experience on the Damascus road *(see Acts 9:1–9)*, but we have to bear in mind that our evidence for that does not actually come from Paul himself, but from Luke, the author of the book of Acts. As far as the vision described in the book of Revelation is concerned, it is much too mystical in style for us to make any assessment of its factual accuracy.

Paul, in the passage already identified above, provides a list of those to whom the risen Christ is said to have appeared:

> '*... he appeared to Cephas (Peter), then to the twelve. Then he appeared to more than five hundred brothers and sisters at one time, most of whom are still alive, though some have died. Then he appeared to James, then to all the apostles ...*' *(1 Corinthians 15:5ff)*

We have no other record of some of these appearances, and it is not altogether clear where Paul received this tradition: he simply says that he had 'received it', which must mean that it was hearsay.

The body of the risen Christ

If a closer study of the accounts of Christ's resurrection appearances leads us to feel a little uncertain about their factual accuracy, then that uncertainty may be heightened by the ways in which the risen Jesus is described. Mark's Gospel can be set aside here, because it stops short at the point where the grave is found to be empty, and neither of the two alternative endings is Mark's own work. There are no resurrection appearances at all in Mark's book. In Matthew's Gospel the risen Jesus is said to have appeared 'suddenly' *(Matthew 28:9)*, suggesting an experience in which 'one moment he was not there, and the next moment he was'. Luke's Gospel tells us that when the two disciples met Jesus on the road to Emmaus,

> *'... their eyes were kept from recognizing him ...'*
> *(Luke 24:16),*

and, in the fourth Gospel, the author records that when Mary visited the empty tomb she saw the risen Jesus, but mistook him for the gardener *(John 20:15)*. In the same Gospel, Jesus is said to have met with his disciples by entering a room despite the fact that the doors were firmly locked *(see John 20:19 and 26)*.

What are we to make of all this? Christian tradition has frequently tried to deal with it by saying that Christ's resurrection body was necessarily 'different' from his earthly body, but always in an unspecified way. What we have to bear in mind, of course, is that in the New Testament period there were several different points of view in circulation about the nature of the human body. There was the Greek way of thinking, in which a human being was thought to be a physical body containing a spirit or soul within it: according to this theory, at death the physical body decayed and was destroyed, but the inner spirit or soul was released to continue existing in a 'disembodied' way. Over against this, there was the Hebrew (Jewish) way of thinking, in which a human being was looked upon as an inseparable combination of physical and spiritual elements – as a 'body-soul'. At creation, God had breathed his life-giving spirit into humankind, and thus made a 'living being' *(see Genesis 2:7)*. The spiritual aspect could not be removed without destroying the physical – hence the plea found in the Old Testament:

> *'Do not cast me away from your presence, and do not take your holy spirit from me ...'* (Psalm 51:11)

To the Hebrew mind, there could be no such thing as a 'spiritual resurrection' which did not also involve the physical body. The spirit and the body were 'all of a piece', and indeed this is the kind of thinking which lay behind the belief that one's spiritual life must of necessity be evidenced in one's actual physical behaviour. Within the New Testament we can see the inevitable tension which existed between these two views of the nature of humankind. In the context of our discussion, however, we should note that traditional Old Testament religious thought could not cope with belief in a resurrection which did not also include the raising of the body. As a former Archbishop of Canterbury once observed, what is purely spiritual is negligible – it cannot *do* anything.

The contribution of Paul

We might find that the thinking of St Paul is helpful here. As we have already seen, although throughout his letters he generally avoided making any direct reference to the human Jesus, he did like to use the imagery of the Christian Church as constituting the 'body of Christ' here on earth:

> *'For in the one Spirit we were all baptized into one body – Jews or Greeks, slaves or free – and we were all made to drink of one Spirit. Indeed, the body does not consist of one member, but of many ... Now you are the body of Christ and individually members of it ...'* (1 Corinthians 12:13 and 27)

It is the existence of the Church, physically present on earth and conjoined with Christ as it shares in the gift of the Spirit, which is, for Paul the 'proof' of the resurrection. He never suggests that Christian faith is derived from speculating about an empty grave: it comes rather from experiencing the presence of the risen Christ and from sharing in the new life which his death made possible. This kind of thinking may well have come to Paul from his experience on the Damascus road *(see Acts*

9:1–9). We cannot be certain of this, of course, because the experience is described not by Paul himself, but by Luke. However, it is interesting to note than when Paul fell to the ground during that strange event, he asked who it was who was speaking to him, and he heard a voice saying:

> *'I am Jesus, whom you are persecuting ...' (Acts 9:5)*

But as far as he knew he was not persecuting Jesus. Jesus was dead. He was persecuting the Christian community – the Church. It perhaps came to him then that the Church was indeed to be identified with Christ, representing his physical form in the world. This may well be pure speculation, of course, but it points in the direction of Paul's special insight about the evidence of the resurrection being found most plainly in the existence of the fellowship of Christian believers.

Certainly Paul looked upon Christians as people who had died and risen with Christ, and who were now enjoying a new life in him:

> *'For if we have been united with him in a death like his, we will certainly be united with him in a resurrection like his. We know that our old self was crucified with him so that the body of sin might be destroyed, and we might no longer be enslaved to sin. (Romans 6:5–6)*

In our final Study we will examine this idea more closely.

POINTS FOR DISCUSSION

1. If Jesus rose bodily from the grave, this does not mean that he would have to die all over again later on?
2. How can the resurrection of Jesus's physical body be of any advantage to us?
3. Do you find the evidence for the resurrection very convincing, especially in the light of what modern science tells us about the nature of life and death?

4. Is there any force in the claim that the story of the resurrection is really a 'happy ending' which the early Church felt compelled to proclaim in order to save face after the crucifixion of Jesus?

5. If Jesus rose physically from the dead, why did he seem to be unrecognisable to some of those who saw him and had previously known him intimately?

6. What do you think St Paul meant when he referred to the Christian Church as 'the body of Christ'? Was he talking about Christ's resurrected body, or did he just mean 'the company of those who follow Christ'?

8 | Risen With Christ

It is one thing to claim that Jesus died and then rose again from the dead: but it is quite another thing to say that his death and resurrection can somehow be relevant to the whole of the human race. This is the point at which many people find serious difficulties with their Christian faith. They can acknowledge that Jesus's *teachings* have a universal application, and they can see how his *life* might be used as an example for others to follow; but they cannot see how one man's personal experience of death and resurrection can genuinely be shared with others. Certainly it is possible to believe that Jesus lived and died, and equally certainly it is possible to believe that in some miraculous way he still lives. But it is extremely hard to see how anyone else can participate in all this, or benefit from it. To be identified in this way with Christ would surely mean that we would somehow have to be 'in him', and he would have to be 'in us'. Such a possibility seems at first to be quite absurd.

Yet this is exactly what traditional Christianity has always taught. Paul set out this principle very clearly in several places in his letters, where he affirmed that a Christian is someone who is 'in Christ', and who has Christ 'in himself': for example,

> 'Do you not know that all of us who have been baptized into Christ Jesus were baptized into his death? Therefore we have been buried with him by baptism into death, so that, just as Christ was raised from the dead by the glory of the Father, so we too might walk in newness of life.' (Romans 6:3–4)

> '... Christ has been raised from the dead, the first fruits of those who have died. For since death came through a human being, the resurrection of the dead has also come through a human being; for as all die in Adam, so all will be made alive in Christ.' (1 Corinthians 15:20–22)

> *'I have been crucified with Christ; and it is no longer I who live, but it is Christ who lives in me. And the life I now live in the flesh I live by faith in the Son of God, who loved me and gave himself for me ...' (Galatians 2:20)*

The common life

This concept of participation in the life, death and resurrection of Christ seems foreign to the modern western mind, but perhaps it will seem a little less alien when it is set in the context of eastern thought. As we have shown earlier, one of the special insights of the Hebrew world was its awareness that human beings are not isolated from each other, but rather share in a common nature *(see Lenten Study 1)*. Human nature was understood to be 'corporate', though not at the expense of true individuality. People could be distinct and private individuals, but they were, by their very origin, also part of each other. They were all bound up in the one 'bundle of life'.

Christian love

The concept of corporate humanity therefore points the way towards a deeper understanding of what is meant by 'sharing' in Christ's death and resurrection. But it does not take us all the way. Another important Christian principle which is directly relevant here is that of **agape** ('love'). Christian love is understood as that quality within someone which makes him/her able to identify closely and sympathetically with someone else, to such an extent that joys and burdens can be shared. Paul likened this to the way in which the human body is put together:

> *'If one member suffers, all suffer together with it; if one member is honoured, all rejoice together with it.'*
> *(1 Corinthians 12:26)*

It is this special kind of love which prompts a person to forget self, and to be able to stand in someone else's shoes. It is the impulse to hand over oneself to the loved one. It expresses itself in acts of self-giving and self-sharing:

> *'If you abide in me, and my words abide in you, ask for whatever you wish, and it will be done for you ... No-one has greater love than this, to lay down one's life for one's friends.'*
> *(John 15:7ff)*

Conversely, to receive this special kind of love is at the same time to receive not only the love itself but also the one who does the loving. When we genuinely love someone, we actually give ourselves away to that person. What this kind of love does is to create a bond between the lover and the loved – a bond so complete that they are no longer two, but one.

In all this we are touching upon something which almost defies words. It is no accident that, throughout history, whenever people have tried to express genuine love, they have found it necessary to break out of the conventions of ordinary practical language and move into poetry or song. They have also commonly found that love is a painful as well as an enjoyable experience, because it involves the recognition that they are not, after all, the only people in the world who matter. Love completely destroys selfishness, and in so doing it destroys that pride which makes us think that we are superior to all others. The English novelist Iris Murdoch put it very succinctly:

> *'Love is the extremely difficult realisation that something other than oneself is real. Love, and so art and morals, is the discovery of reality'.* (Iris Murdoch, **The Sublime and the Good**, *published in* **Chicago Review** *1959)*

To participate in Christ's death and resurrection is an act of love and an act of faith. It requires that the would-be Christian shall 'put away self' *(see Romans 6:6)* in order to allow for the entry of what St Paul calls 'the new life of the Spirit' *(see Romans 7:6)*.

Being 'in Christ': Christian baptism

As we saw in the passage quoted above from Paul's letter to the Romans, the outward mode or expression of being 'in Christ' is traditionally associated with the doctrine of Christian Baptism. Baptism is the sacramental symbol of the crucifixion of the old self, and of receiving new life from Christ. It is a process of dying and rising again. It is not an expression of *our* dedication to Christ, but of *his* dedication to us. Of course, it involves a readiness on our part to receive what is offered, but it is not in itself a voluntary or a conditional agreement. It places the Christian within the fellowship of Christ's body, the Church, and at the same time it is an acknowledgement that to be 'in Christ' is to be a member of a corporate body. Thus a Christian takes very seriously the principle that, when Christ draws us into himself through his divine love, we become members of an all-embracing fellowship, in which

> *'we do not live to ourselves, and we do not die to ourselves. If we live, we live to the Lord, and if we die, we die to the Lord; so then, whether we live or whether we die, we are the Lord's.'*
> *(Romans 14:7–8)*

Christ in us: feeding on Christ

If Christian Baptism is the mode of entry into the body of Christ, and of belonging to the corporate fellowship of Christian believers, then the Sacrament of Holy Communion (sometimes called the Eucharist or the Mass) represents the way in which Christians are sustained within that fellowship. We are 'in Christ' by virtue of belonging to the Church, and he is 'in us' because he feeds his people, just as a loving father ensures that his children are properly nourished. Furthermore, we are 'in one another', in the sense that Christians express their unity by the exercise of that very love which holds them together and make them one in Christ.

According to the fourth Gospel, Jesus used this kind of 'being-in' language when he was explaining to his disciples how it was that he and God could genuinely be 'one':

> *'Whoever has seen me has seen the Father. How can you say 'Show us the Father'? Do you not believe that I am in the*

Father and the Father is in me? The words that I say to you I do not speak on my own; but the Father who dwells in me does his works. Believe me that I am in the Father and the Father is in me ...' (John 14:8ff)

This is said in the context of love:

'On that day you will know that I am in my Father, and you in me, and I in you. They who have my commandments and keep them are those who love me; and those who love me will be loved by my Father, and I will love them and reveal myself to them ...' (John 14:20–21),

making it plain that, in the final analysis, it is love which brings people into Christ and which holds them together in him.

It is therefore perfectly understandable that, when St Paul had finished explaining the essence of his understanding of the Christian Gospel and of how Christ is 'in us' and we are 'in him', he should then go on to expound the nature of the Christian life itself. He shows that it is now no longer a selfish kind of life, in which 'charity begins at home', but a sacrificial kind of life, in which everyone lives for the sake of everyone else. The strong are not there to overpower the weak, but to strengthen them. The rich are set within the Church to help the poor, the learned are to teach the unlearned, and those who are advanced in faith are to support those who have only just begun their journey. Everyone's life is offered to everyone else. This is what Paul meant when he addressed himself to the Corinthians on the subject of being undivided *(see 1 Corinthians 12)*, and it is certainly what he meant when he set out his interpretation of love as the greatest of all Christian virtues. It was also at the forefront of his mind when he wrote to the Galatians and told them that

'... those who belong to Christ have crucified the flesh with its passions and desires ... Let us not become conceited, competing against one another, envying one another.' (Galatians 5:24–26)

Those who live in constant rivalry have not understood what it is to belong to the one body: nor have they understood what it is to have died and risen with Christ. To share in Christ's resurrection is to live in a new way, putting oneself aside for the good of others, and allowing one's own life to be merged into the common life.

POINTS FOR DISCUSSION

1. What do you understand to be happening when someone receives Christian Baptism?
2. How does a Christian 'receive Christ' in the sacrament of Holy Communion (the Eucharist or Mass)? Is this simply a symbolic act?
3. What is the difference between 'attending Church' and being a confirmed member of the Church?
4. What are the marks of Christian love? How is it recognised?
5. What did Paul mean when he said that a Christian neither lives nor dies to himself alone?
6. If our 'old self' is destroyed at Baptism, and we receive Christ's new life, does that mean that we will never again experience temptation or failure?
7. Is it a Christian principle that we must *never* compete with one another in any circumstances? If not, what did Paul mean when he told the Galatians that they must not become conceited nor compete against one another *(Galatians 5:26)*?

INDEX OF BIBLICAL REFERENCES

OLD TESTAMENT

Genesis 1:1ff   *page* 46
1:1—2:4a   13, 67
1:26ff   14
2:4ff   5, 13, 67, 75, 97
2:7   112
2:21ff   68
3   15
3:8   5
3:14–19   75
3:19   67
18:25   83
21:1ff   35
37:11   41

Exodus 1:22ff   32
3:1ff   7, 8
12:12ff   91
13:11ff   91
14:19–20   8
19:1ff   22
19:12–13   9
19:21   9
33:19   84
34:1ff   22

Leviticus 5:14–16   91
17:11   91

Numbers 32:23   69

Deuteronomy 16:10   90
18:15   22
21:22–23   103
29:2–4   9

Ruth 3:9   37

1 Samuel 1:1ff   91
1:20ff   36
2:1ff   38
3:1ff   8
3:2–14   8
15:22   93

2 Samuel 7:12ff   24
8:15   83

2 Chronicles 30:9   84

Job 1:9–11   77
2:3   77
42:1ff   78

Psalm 2:4   6
8:3–4   7
8:4–5   14
10:1   6
18:16   6
22   103
22:1   104
23:4   6
50:6   82
51:11   113
69   103
69:21   104
69:23   104
86:15   85
91:7ff   77
139:1–18   7

Proverbs 15:20   98
23:22   98

Isaiah 7:14   30
10:5ff   76
11:1–16   25
13:11   84
40:2   76
53   100, 103
53:5–11   79, 100
53:7   104

Jeremiah 1:11–19   10
30:19ff   36
31:31ff   22
33:14–15   25

Ezekiel 16:8   37
18:2ff   71
18:19–20   71

Hosea 3:5   25
4:9   84
6:6   93
11:1   32, 68, 98

Reference	Page
Amos 5:11	83
5:21ff	83
7:1ff	10
8:1–3	11
9:11	25
Micah 6:8	83
Habakkuk 1:13	78
3:17	78

NEW TESTAMENT

Reference	Page
Matthew 1:2–16	25
1:16	26, 29
1:18–25	30, 36
1:20	49
1:21	30, 60
2:1	26
2:7–15	23
2:13–14	31, 32
2:19	31
2:23	32
4:1ff	54
5:1—7:29	23
5:7	85
11:29	96
26:39	100
26:57	102
26:65–66	102
27:13ff	102
27:37	103
27:57–60	103
27:64	105
28:1ff	108
28:13–14	108
28:19	109
Mark 1:9–11	45
8:22–26	9
5:39	105
8:27–30	9
8:33	96
14:32–50	102
14:36	100
15:1–5	104
15:1–47	103, 105
15:24	104
15:26	103
15:33	104
15:36	104
16:1ff	108
Luke 1:5	39
1:11ff	36
1:17	36
1:24–25	35
1:26ff	36, 37
1:26—2:52	35
1:30ff	60
1:35	49
1:46–56	38
1:67–69	38
1:68–75	21
2:1	39
2:9	37
2:11	61
2:16	41
2:19	41
2:21–24	41
2:29–32	38–41
2:41–51	31, 41
4:1ff	54
6:36	85
15:11ff	99
15:29	99
15:31	99
15:32	99
22:42	100
22:43	37
23:39	103
23:55	105
24:1ff	108
24:13ff	110
24:16	112
24:21	106
24:28ff	110
John 1:6–9	26, 45
1:1–18	45
1:11	33
1:12–13	46
1:14	46
1:14–18	19
1:15	45
1:19–31	26
1:44	10
2:1–11	47
2:15	96
3:1ff	47, 49
4:16	80
4:34	100
5:1–18	47
5:19	47
5:21	48
5:22	48

5:30	100	8:12–14	47
5:27	48	12:19	84
6:41–42	48	13:1–2	97
7:41–42	44	14:7–8	119
8:12ff	48		
8:19	48	1 Corinthians 9:1	111
9:1–41	47	11:17ff	93
9:2	76	12	120
14:7	48	12:4ff	55
14:8ff	120	12:12ff	72, 113
14:9–10	48	12:26	70, 117
14:20–21	120	13:8	55, 71
14:25–26	49	15:3ff	52, 111
15:7	118	15:8	111
15:13	80	15:20–22	116
15:26	49	15:22	17
16:15	99		
19:19	103	2 Corinthians 1:3ff	56
20:1ff	108, 109	4:5–7	56
20:15	112	5:16	52
20:19–26	112	5:18ff	87
20:28	48	5:19	53
20:31	45	13:5	56
21:1ff	109		
		Galatians 2:20	117
Acts 5:19	37	5:24–26	120
9:1–9	114		
10:3	37	Philippians 2:5–11	53
12:7	37	2:6ff	16
Romans 1:3–4	106	Colossians 1:15ff	16, 53, 54
3:23	70	1:17	55
5:1–5	72	2:9	53, 54
5:6	20	3:1ff	56
5:10	87		
5:12	70	Hebrews 4:15	18
5:17	17	5:5–6	93
6:1ff	55	7:23–24	94
6:3–4	116	7:26ff	93
6:5–6	114, 118	9:11	94
6:9	20	10:8ff	94
6:11	55	10:10	79
6:17ff	23		
7:4	20	James 2:1–4	83
7:6	118	2:13	85
8:3	23, 52		
8:9–11	20	Revelation 1:13	111